Miraculous Interventions VII

The Saving of America

Deborah Aubrey-Peyron

Books by
Deborah Aubrey-Peyron

Miraculous Interventions	(2011)
Christmas Chaos!	(2011)
Miraculous Interventions II	(2012)
Modern Day Priests, Prophets,	
Pastors & Everyday Visionaries	
Miraculous Interventions III	(2014)
2012 The Miraculous Year	
My Story, Richard Riddell Mosely	(2014)
My Faith Journey	(2015)
Miracles I Have Experienced	
Dennis Murphy	
Let's Take a Walk, Dave	(2015)
The Story of David Becker	
A Man Who Just Believed God	
An Old Man's Christmas	(2015)
By Deborah Aubrey-Peyron and	
Ronald J. Aubrey	
Illustrated by Shane Aubrey, BA	
Christmas Chaos! Coloring Book	(2015)
Miraculous Interventions IV	(2016)
The Gathering Season	
Miraculous Interventions	(2016)
The Best of Miraculous Interventions	
Deb's Christmas Cookbook	(2016)
A Collection of Recipes from	
Four Generations of Family	
& Friends...plus stories!	
He Will Always Be My Sunshine	(2017)
Co-written with Lisa Wisdom	

Book by Ronald J. Aubrey,
Edited by Deborah Aubrey-Peyron

Miraculous Interventions VII

The Saving of America

Deborah Aubrey-Peyron

Home Crafted Artistry & Printing
New Albany, Indiana

Copyright 2018 by Deborah Aubrey-Peyron.
All rights reserved.
Published by Home Crafted Artistry & Printing, 2018 with permission.

ISBN-13: 978-0-9974347-7-4
ISBN-10: 0-9974347-7-5

Home Crafted Artistry & Printing
1252 Beechwood Avenue
New Albany, IN 47150

All of Mrs. Peyron's books are available on the web at:
www.HomeCraftedArtistry@yahoo.com

Author Contact Information:
E-mail peyronsinjesus@yahoo.com
Special discounts are available on quantity purchases of 25 or more copies. Speaking or book-signing engagements may be arranged upon request. Please, E-mail or write to the above address.

Cover design by Mary Dow Bibb Smith and Deborah Aubrey-Peyron.
Scripture quote is from Matthew 10:27.
Proudly printed in the United States of America.

Dedication

For America, the country I love. One
prayer, as the angels put it well, over 2,000
years ago, "......peace on earth to men of good
will."

This is my personal prayer:
That all people would come to faith in
Jesus Christ, Yeshua Ben Elohim, the Messiah,
so that He may come back in glory and in
peace – without any destruction.
Yet, Thy will be done, Lord.

(This author has read The Book of
Revelation. And I understand this prayer does
not line up with the prophecies written in it.
This is not to discount those warnings. I am
simply sharing a prayer from a mother's heart.
I fully understand – it is His will, not mine,
that will be done.)

Acknowledgments

As always, I couldn't do this without the love and guidance of our Heavenly Father, as well as my precious husband, Mark, and my publisher of 10 years and best friend of 25 years, Mary Dow Smith. What a wreck I would be without any of you!

The farther down this path I have gone, the more I understand my life is not my own. It belongs to a far-grander scheme than any I could think of.

My mother must've named me correctly:

Deborah: a judge and warrior

Anne: Mary's momma, full of love, understanding and compassion.

Somewhere, in the middle of all these, I too, am.

> *"Beloved,*
> *I wish above all things*
> *that thou mayest prosper and be in health,*
> *even as thy soul prospereth."*
> 3rd John 2:2

Love,

Deb

Table of Contents

Introduction

I didn't see "MI VI, Warn Those Who Will Listen" coming. I wasn't going to write it. I was not going to tell or warn any or all (in the public) who would listen...but my editor and publisher Mary Dow Smith would have it no other way.

"Deb! You have to write it!" She cried out.

I responded loudly, "I don't have enough time to write it, Mary!"

It was an out and out fight.

I went on in case she didn't hear me the first time, "Conference starts in four weeks! That would give me — at best — three weeks to write it!" Surely, Mary would see reason.

Did I mention I was speaking to my publisher? Sympathy has not always been one of her best assets — at least not with me.

Without missing a beat, or batting an eye, Mary replied, "Then you better get started."

I sighed. I had just lost the battle — thank God. For Mary was listening closer to Our Lord than I was.

At the same time I was pulling it all together to start, an equally intriguing title came to me. I thought it was the subtitle to book VI. Well, that was probably wishful thinking on my part.

But it gave me hope for our future. And the further down the path we got for *The Saving of America*, the more dangerous the times became.

I Warned Those Who Would Listen
A brief recap

Ever since the first warning--almost four years earlier, from Pastor David Becker in Lexington, Kentucky, of a possible nuclear strike from a rouge nation on American soil, I had an eerie feeling about his prophecy. I promised Dave that until I received verification of his prophecy, I would tell no one. But if the day ever came that I indeed verified his word of knowledge, I would tell everyone who would listen to me.

Verification came the spring of 2017, at a seminar in Louisville, Kentucky from a visiting couple from Rochester, New York. Their names were John and Carol Leary. As Carol and I confirmed the same prophecy from two different people, we knew our lives had just been joined together for a greater cause than ourselves.

I told my doctor, our local law enforcement officials, and I shared my information with local pastors and national pastors. All from May through September of 2017. And we prayed— hard—that I had done everything God expected of me. That I had gotten it all right. And I dreamed, boy did I dream.

A Nuclear Vision
(August 5th, 2017)

[Taken mostly, from book:
*Miraculous Interventions VI,
Warn Those Who Will Listen*]

"It was early in the morning. I am still not sure if this was indeed a vision or a dream; it came out of a mist. I could see Mark and me sleeping in bed together—peacefully sleeping.

Through closed eyes, I saw an instantaneous brilliant flash of light—it was gone in an eighth of a second—like lightening. My heart sank and I cried as I waited for the percussion of the nuclear blast to hit.

In this vision, I turned toward the clock, it was 8:15 a.m.

I realized then, I was actually turned the other way in bed—opposite of the way I saw me in the vision. When I turned over, I saw it was 7:45 a.m. But just like in the vision, I was crying.

Mark and I prayed against nuclear war from that day on—especially against the rouge country of North Korea."

I hoped and prayed God would send me a sign that my message got to all those it was sent to—especially the letter I sent to a pastor who had a date at the White House. Toward the end of August, at a church service, a word of knowledge came down the pipe from a visiting pastor.

As Apostle Larry was finishing his service, he stopped, then paced back and forth at the front of the altar.

He said, "There is someone here who had a message. And a person of influence is going to a person of great influence with your message. They will remember you. Just like the butler remembered Joseph to Potiphar, you will be remembered too."

He asked who this message was for, because God told him that person would need prayer! I raised my hand and he came running and prayed over me and for all who were around us.

I was also hopeful, later that fall, when Mark and I went on vacation, while in Tennessee, I would get a second confirmation.

And that is where this book takes off from. The rest of the story...

To Start the Days of Elul
Something about BJ
(Last week of August, 2017)

The Lord let me know in His way, I could have the last week of August off, to rest up between books.

I thought, "Oh, boy! Just a relaxing week! No messages, no Words of Knowledge or visions."

Nothing but rest....

And I was right. There weren't any — for me. After all, we had just finished a three-week push in the Spirit against a nuclear attack—which I knew was imminent, unless stopped.

But what I forgot to ask about—or to include—was my husband, Mark.

So that week began...

Mark came home from work on a Monday evening with a perplexed look on his face.

"What's wrong?" I asked as he washed his hands for dinner.

"Uuummm," Mark answered, shaking his head from side to side. "Something's wrong," he muttered.

I went immediately into "warrior" mode.

"With the world?! With the world?! Is it a nuclear strike?!" I was ready at the helm.

"No, no. Closer to us than that." Mark was still pondering.

Then I went over our children and their children.

"Ben, Davey, Andy?! Their wives, or our grandchildren, Lily, Mattie, Sophie or Edward?! Is it that close to us?!" My heart was already pounding.

Irritation began to creep in to Mark's spirit and voice.

"No, not that close. Close to us but not that close."

"Mom! Have you called Mom?!" Ready to panic in three, two, one...

Mark's overly-helpful wife had now gotten on his last nerve.

"Someone would have called us if it was Mom!" Big sigh!

He paused.

"I sent BJ a text."

"Ohhhhh....."

Within one minute of Mark stating his concern about his youngest sister, she was calling. As Mark told her about his concern for her, she broke down crying. Yes, she'd had a hard week. And BJ was mad....*was* mad. The Lord had dealt with her, and she needed to tell her story.

BJ owns a plant and garden nursery. While she was watering plants, a cicada was bothering her. Really bothering her.

The Lord God spoke. "Do you hear how annoying the sound of the cicada is to you?"

"Yes, Lord." BJ responded.

"That is how you have sounded to me this past weekend."

19

BJ immediately stopped. Anger and resentment fell off of her like water. Mercy replaced them.

"Oh, how good and merciful God is to us," She started. "He spoke to me and had you confirm it. Thank you Mark for being so obedient to God."

Mark and I were all smiles.

"Your welcome, little sister, you are welcome...."

Apocalyptic Events
(The **first week** of September, 2017)

1. Deb Grimes called late one evening to tell me North Korea had just sent a message with the exact words to the White House that had been in my warning dream on June 30th.*

Deb said, "North Korea says they are sending gift packages to America September 7th!"

Prayers went up.

2. September 8th, a noted Indiana pastor with an online YouTube church, Paul Begley reported an earthquake of an 8.0 magnitude in San Francisco, Mexico. He wondered, could it have been part of the warning about an earthquake in San Francisco, we assumed was SF California?

3. I had seen in a vision dream, (back in August) what I thought were oriental people from a large land mass (I thought China, still possibly is) having a huge earthquake. I saw the fear on their faces, and their land split like a river ran through it.

Prayers went up because one never knows...or can one?

I pondered, "What did the rest of September, 2017 hold? Would there be an

---

* *In my dream, he said, "I brought you a package for your birthday." What was reported that he said was, "I'm sending a package for your birthday."*
See Miraculous Interventions VI, Warn Those Who Will Listen, *page 132* "An Early Morning Hour"

attempted nuclear attack? Did the fires and smoke all across our nation – as Pastor David Becker had seen in a vision – indicate, as he had wondered, that Yellowstone was going to blow? Or could he have pre-seen the fires that started in California and were now so large that the smoke made it all the way to St. Louis, Missouri?"

Even the secular public knew something was in the air, no pun intended. Sales of pre-packaged foods, camping equipment, and medical supplies skyrocketed.

Now, if only we could stop it, God permitting....

September of 2017 had not been kind to America, or the world, for that matter.

A whole host of states in the United States were battling fires, to include:
California
Oregon
Washington State
Montana and others

Other countries were battling their own waves of death and destruction as well. British Columbia, Alberta, Canada, Nova Scotia, Greece, Brazil, Portugal, Algeria, Tunisia, Greenland, Siberia and the Sakha Republic of Russia were also being consumed acres at a time by fires, many of unknown origin.

Surely, this was what the prophet David Wilkerson, and our own dear friend and prophet—David Becker saw in visions of their own, set apart by 30 years.

A triple-digit heat wave dubbed "lucifer" (of all names!) swept through the European countries of Italy, France, Spain, Switzerland, Hungary, Poland, Romania, Bosnia, Croatia, and Serbia.

Southern California also fought triple-digit heat that smashed down all-time record highs of 115 degrees. News stories showed people sweltering as they walked to their vehicles.

By mid-September, Yellowstone had rumbled with a series of earthquakes and tremors (hundreds) that made even the heartiest souls think the East Coast looked like a good move for safety.

Japan, Mexico, and Australia suffered huge earthquakes registering 6.1, 7.2 and 8.1 respectively. The earthquake that hit San Francisco, Mexico receded beach lines by 50 plus meters.

And then, there was the all-time record-breaking Hurricane Harvey versus Houston with over 50 inches of rain. Devastation of a nuclear capacity had hit Texas.

If that wasn't enough, Hurricane Irma took direct aim at the **whole state** of Florida at category five. Not to mention going on at the same time, the largest CME* flare from our sun ever recorded.

At the time, I wondered, if there was such a thing as Mother Nature, had she really gone mad.

* CME = Coronal Mass Ejection.

23

A Storm on the Horizon of Epic Proportions
The entire state of Florida, USA
(September 8-11th, 2017)

At the same time Mark and I were putting out (proverbial) fires around us—no deference to the states out west that really were dealing with unprecedented fires on their own—another storm that threatened devastation it its wake was brewing.

NOAA ["National Oceanic and Atmospheric Administration] watched the storm system that came off the coast of Africa take an almost purposeful aim at the islands between Cuba and North America. The area they originated from, off the African coastal waters, was known for creating super-storms of "Biblical" proportions, real land destroyers. As it crossed the ocean, picking up speed and mass, warnings started all over Cuba, the Virgin Islands and the whole Eastern North American coastline.

Hurricane Irma was four times larger than the destructive Hurricane Matthew of 2016. How on earth could that happen?!

I wondered, were our earth weather systems being influenced by HAARP [High Frequency Active Auroral Research Program] – which may have been influenced by the demons of the nether world? [Search this on Youtube for information on this subject.] Or was it truly a warning system? Was God trying to get our world's attention any and every which way He could...?

September 4th, Irma strengthened to a category-4 hurricane over the Atlantic – then, upgraded to a category-5 with winds of 185 mph as it approached land. Irma made its first landfall over the Caribbean Island of Barbuda. Every single building was destroyed and all its 1600 inhabitants were left homeless.

Over the next three days, Irma centered west over Anguilla, St. Martin, St. Bart's and both British and US Virgin Islands. The damage was catastrophic. Ninety percent of the buildings on several of the islands were damaged or destroyed. Irma brushed the coast of Puerto Rico and left one million residents without power. Irma then passed just shy of the Dominican Republic and Haiti. It caused widespread flooding before aiming at the Turks and Caicos Islands in the Bahamas. Irma maintained at Category-5 strength for three days—breaking all records in the satellite era.

And it was on a direct collision course with the entire state of Florida. In its first wake was Cuba. Irma hit Cuba with 160 mph winds at landfall on Camaguey Archipelago late Friday evening.

This same Friday evening at our home was when we were starting our opening prayers with John and Carol Leary. With the many words of knowledge we had all been receiving before then, we had arranged a conference for this weekend.

Mark and I let people know of the conference with John and Carol on Friday at our home, Saturday with Fr. David at the Knights of Columbus Hall, continuing informally at our home on Sunday – which, incidentally, continued into Tuesday!

People were drawn from the north, south, east and west! Could we please save them a seat?

Why sure!

That Ran Right into an Epic Weekend!
(September 8-11th, 2017)

As Irma got closer and closer to landfall on the eastern seaboard, prayer warriors were all gathering at our home in Southern Indiana. People came from all over. Almost 100 of them arrived from seven states on that Friday evening.

And we were headed for a fight with destructive forces.

Don't worry, saints, we were used to winning....

"Do you think we've made enough food?" I asked my compatriots Katie Yocum, Deb Grimes and Mary Smith.

Between the three-day conference totals, we would be feeding over 100 people breakfast, lunch and dinner.

"I think we will be fine, Deb," Katie reasoned. She and Deb Grimes were always the calm warriors. I was, and am, the jumper.

Mark was on his way to the Louisville International Airport to pick up John and Carol Leary, and their friend, Linda who would be meeting Fr. David that afternoon at our home.

I set out our fall decorum as we waited for our company to arrive. And of course, when they walked into our home, I was the one with my hands in dish water.

They were introduced to everyone else first. It went something like this:

"Hi! I'm Katie!"

"Hi! I'm Debbie!"

"Ohhh! Debbie!"

"Uh, Debbie Grimes! I'm not the lady of the house."

Drying off my hands, I said, "Here I am. Welcome to our home."

Since I knew John and Carol, I said, "You must be Linda."

Again, "Ohhhh, Debbie! It's so nice to finally meet you!"

Of course, hugs and smiles were exchanged all around. Carol gave me a hug that felt like it was from a long-lost friend. We showed our New England friends to their bedrooms and allowed them time to settle in. I set out snacks for everyone until it was time to go out for lunch. Dinner was still cooking....

Conversations over fish and fries went quickly to the deep things of God, and concern for those in the wake of Irma. I let our company know we had children and grandchildren smack in the middle of the state, staying at a Walt Disney World resort for safety.

I had let Andy, our youngest, know we would be lifting them all up in prayer for the whole weekend. His response to me was, "Momma, do you think God has forgotten that we still live in Florida?"

Thomas Andrew's complete faith was on it.

The weekend events were set...or so I thought.

Friday evening, John Leary was scheduled to speak at our home. Saturday, Fr. David would be speaking at the Knights of Columbus Hall in Lanesville, Indiana, on the topic of the Immaculate Heart of Mary, all day until 4 that afternoon.

We assumed Sunday would be a day of rest and thanksgiving. Fr. David and Linda would be leaving that afternoon. John and Carol had scheduled to go back home on Monday evening.

Well, so much for the plans we could see. God's plans and ways are always much higher than ours. And longer....

We all agreed we would begin and end the evening with prayer for Florida. When Fr. David arrived Friday afternoon, he joined in with offering two masses for everyone in Irma's path. Divine Mercy Chaplets were said over and over for the same intention.

If you could force a weather system into submission through prayer, we were well on our way to doing just that.

Friday evening I prepared three roasts for dinner, supplied by Katie Yocum. It had all the trimmings and was several of our guests' favorite meal of the weekend.

The Gospel of
John and Carol
(September 8-12th, 2017)

As dinner wound down, people started arriving for John and Carol's talk. We were able to seat 50 in our basement. There were a few ladies that could not navigate steps, so we compromised for their situation and came up with a great idea! I called Carol's phone and we put them both on speaker. Her phone was at the podium where John was speaking. I ran my phone upstairs to the waiting women in our sunroom. They were ecstatic! They weren't left out at all! I was sure it was a divine inspiration.

John opened the three-hour meeting with a prayer for the people in Texas and Florida, those suffering in the wake of one hurricane and the impending landing of the other!

He opened with a warning against powers that be who wanted to take our guns. He also gave an update on refuges across the United States.

John spoke on warnings of major events to pray against. After all, prayer can stop a lot of things except one thing — God's will. Even our prayers cannot stop that. But everything else is fair game.

John spoke of the life-review and mini-judgments he felt were coming. He warned not to take the chip in our hand or forehead no matter what they tell you. And if you think they will never pass that law, they already did. It was written into the Obama Care Bill.

John was also told by the power of the Holy Spirit, that a world famine was coming. And there would be a great schism in the Roman Catholic Church.

There could also be a crash of the dollar, calling for martial law to be set up as a possible dictatorship. Along with this, there could be major disruptions in services and supplies— just like in Venezuela.

John also felt there was an antichrist figure waiting in the wings (2017-2018) ready to take the world stage. Because of him, John felt we were close to the start of the Great Tribulation by merely observing world events. He felt that as these events unfold, he and Carol at 75 years old, would live to see the rise of this man.

John said, in that time-frame, look for a chastisement comet to hit the Atlantic Ocean. It will appear like two suns in the sky. It will be seen on the day of the warning. This is all based on the Book of Revelation and revelation of the Holy Spirit. There will be three days of darkness. The devil will lose the battle and be cast into the Lake of Fire. The Lord God will recreate the earth and Jesus will reign for a long time on the earth. Then we are all Heaven bound as we are purified.

Through August and September of 2017, there have been two category-5 hurricanes, a 50-inch flood, and an 8.1 earthquake in Mexico (prophecy is fulfilling before our eyes). God has told John He will protect His people at the refuges.

When we look to Scripture, we know that the Father in the Old Testament always protected His people before He destroyed the unfaithful. Noah was in the Ark before the flood. In Ezekiel 9, the angels were told not to destroy those with an "X" on their foreheads. In Sodom, again the Lord led Lot and his faithful out before it was destroyed. The Exodus also saw the Israelites led into the desert.

On September 3rd, John received another "download" from the Lord regarding North Korea. Their leader was trying to put war in motion. They detonated a hydrogen bomb underground causing a 6.4 earthquake under the mountain they were in. John felt North Korea could start a conventional war with South Korea and move to an EMP attack on America. It could devastate our land. America wouldn't be able to large-farm produce. Millions would die by starvation.

There is a study/document given to Homeland Security saying the threat of an EMP attack is very real. Up to 90% of Americans could die within one year from no food/mass starvation. No chips would work — cars, trucks, banks, appliances, communication devices, etc.

John asked people to pray very hard that none of this start nor escalate. If it became a nuclear war, millions would die suddenly. He went on to say, this past week, there were black skies over parts of our planet that were not evening-associated. John reiterated to pray for refuges to have enough food, water, heat and shelter throughout this winter.

John also saw in another vision, buildings falling from an earthquake. He saw the San Andreas and the New Madrid faults associated with it. He knew there would be a cluster of earthquakes over the summer in Yellowstone (which, there were.)

John felt these would be a direct result of mortal sins being committed and not being repented of. This country needs more than one day of prayer. We need to repent. We are at the crossroads.

Items John encouraged everyone to buy were: kerosene, warm clothes, water, candles, food, wind-up flash lights, old ringer-type washers (they make those now with foot-pedal power) a camper-stove, a grinder, a propane tank, a one-year supply of all your needs, and a carbon monoxide meter. And make sure, wherever you are, you can get fresh air daily. These items were all for independent survival.

You will also need Spiritual items such as Bibles, rosaries, scapulars, holy water, blessed salt and a Benedict's cross. (Remember, John is speaking to the Catholics and the items they would specifically need.)

John has seen demons come out of people. Evil spirits are attached to addicts, killers, abortionists and their providers, homosexuality, transgender, personality disorders, pornography and the occult. Look at all the people that are suffering. There are demons for all our sins.

John asked, "How can we come against these things? Use blessed salt, the prayer of St. Michael – especially the long form, and holy water."

As John finished that portion of his talk, Carol got up to speak. She spoke on action and involvement. "Get organized! When you have a lot of people at your refuge, give out assignments. Everyone must have responsibilities and chores to do. This will keep order in your area. Make sure you have enough fuel to get through the winter. Have "balances" for stress and high-stress times. When you share distraught times or troubles, you can help each other. When people arrive, they will be distressed."

Carol went on, "Consecrate your property. Whether it be an interim refuge or a large refuge. Angels will bring a shield of invisibility and protection. These will all be helps to you and your group."

John took over from there once again. "In August, I recorded a message that vaccines are causing autism in babies. I am not saying don't get your children vaccinated. I am saying space them out so they don't hurt your children. If you can, avoid flu shots. The side effects are too many. And pray for your children's health."

John paused for a moment, then went on. "I have seen a vision of hell and of purgatory. In hell, I saw the top level were the lukewarm. In the middle, I saw those who sold their souls to satan for fame and fortune. And on the bottom, those who proselytized others to go to hell. The very bottom of purgatory is like hell, but you can get out of there. There are many levels as Jesus is just. The people there need your prayers. There are different levels in each area including heaven."

John also spoke of a priest he knew in Canada. He was in the process of building a monastery. This priest would be holding a couple of conferences in America later that fall. He is a gift for this time, this season.

John mentioned the US dollar —that he saw a change coming. Our passports are already "chipped." At first, they will ask for voluntary chipping of people — then there will be mandatory chipping required. This will be in our bodies.

John strongly advised people not to take the chip for any reason, because they will use it to control people's minds and free will. He expects soon after they start the voluntary chipping, it will become mandatory—especially for the military.

There is a one-world evil and antichrist-spirit out among the people.

Then John told a story.

"St. Maximum Kolbe was in a monastery near the destruction of Nagasaki. Yet his building was not hurt and no one got sick. His Monastery was protected. Fr. Maximum later died in a German Concentration camp giving his life for another man."

John mentioned the possibility of war with North Korea. He said, "Pray to end abortion, and just possibly peace will come with North Korea and they will not start a war. Abortion is the main cause of our judgement."

John asked us if we knew we could fight the devil with prayers and good deeds. He said to ask Jesus to multiply our prayers, too.

I responded, "You know, I never thought of that, but it sure makes good sense." I hoped in my heart, I had gotten it right all along.

John said, "Be watchful of churches and prayer groups being shut down. We are living in tribulation times. Satan and his demons are setting in for a last stand. But God will only allow them to go so far. Satan knows his time is short."

John waited for the effect of his statement to settle in. He went on.

"President Trump is a temporary reprieve. He is God's man. He is trying to turn the tide around. He's fighting the NAFTA treaty, and finish good projects he is starting.

The hands of the clock [indicating the timeline of events] have slowed down. Minutes and hours are fast on our own timelines. But God lives outside of time. [There will be a warning in which] we will see our mini-judgements and then go back to our bodies. This warning is His greatest act of mercy since His death on the cross. Hopefully we will improve our lives and learn from our mistakes."

John paused to gather his next thoughts and took back off again.

"The war and tribulation with the antichrist will only be a short reign. Have no fear. When you see it coming, get to a refuge. Have a backpack ready to leave after the warning. There will be about six weeks for conversion after the warning given."

Comments were made about the Biblical flood of 50 inches of rain in four days with Hurricane Harvey in Texas. It was a destruction that would last a long time. Yet there were many acts of kindness that surfaced. The Cajun Navy from Louisiana showed up and kept hundreds of families from drowning. The goodness of the Lord outshone the destruction of the devil. People experienced God's love through other people's actions and gave it back out to everyone they met.

Toward the end of John and Carol's talks, we were reminded to keep pictures of our family around us. This is requested by our deceased relatives. John spoke about the vibrational energy of the Holy Spirit (just as we have vibrational energy) and said to love God and your neighbor as yourself. Reconcile to all and be saved for the coming battle.

God has helped President Trump to get him where he is today. But, there is a resistance out to get him. It is the "One-World" people who do not like patriots.

John said, "Look for them to first try to impeach him or call him unfit. And if that doesn't work, they may indeed try to kill our duly-elected president."

After that, John started on a completely different topic: purgatory. John has seen purgatory as a grey area. He has seen Heaven and levels of hell. The top level of hell is for those who ignore God. The mid-level of hell is for those who have made bargains with lucifer for fame and fortune. And the last level of hell is for the satanists and luciferians. The mere thought of those places made me shudder.

At John's closing remarks, he touched on each of these—chemtrails are black-ops, since 1998 HAARP has been used to *enhance* hurricanes and earthquakes. There are many refuges in South America and Europe. God is getting His message out about help. CERN [a French acronym – a European Organization for Nuclear Research] is real, and it has satanic rituals attached to it. There are such things as evil rosaries that have curses attached to them. Their crucifixes have serpents on them.

The last thing John said was, "When the time comes, we will all have to drop our phones and electrical devices and head to the refuges."

We closed that portion of the conference with prayers for the people in Cuba and Florida in the direct line of the hurricane. We asked God to take control of the weather and ease it down from a category 5 to one that was survivable for everyone.

I received a call from our women pastors who came all the way from Wisconsin to attend our meetings. Linda and Sherry had arrived at their hotel and wanted me to know they had made it in safely. They would try to make it to part of Saturday's events (which they did) but most definitely would be at our home for dinner that evening.

The thought of Linda and Sherry joining us and our conversations about the imminent return of Jesus brought excitement to my spirit. I could hardly wait to give hugs that next afternoon.

Much to our delight, overnight, the big Category 5 hurricane that destroyed islands and wreaked havoc in Cuba, eased down to 120 mph winds as it headed through the Florida Keys. At the start of Saturday morning, Irma began its turn toward South Florida as we were starting our day for the big conference with Fr. David.

Dark O' Clock

(Saturday September 9th, 2017)

After a late evening of people leaving after 11 p.m., our group cleaned up the kitchen and went to bed after midnight. Mark and I wearily slept on two different couches – upstairs and downstairs. All our beds were filled with guests.

By 5:30 a.m. Saturday morning, I heard the pitter-patter of little priest feet. Fr. David was looking for the coffee maker to make coffee before church at 6 a.m. He smiled sheepishly as I rounded the corner to come to his aid. At that time of the morning, coffee sounded awfully good to me, too.

Fr. David went downstairs to set up for mass as I woke up our other guests. I peeked my head into bedrooms and said softly, "Mass in half an hour!"

Sleepy troops lined up for our two bathrooms. Mumbles of "Hi, hon," came out of Mark's mouth before his eyes opened.

Mass in our home went well. It was so peaceful—like it was the way it was supposed to be. As if God was watching our little group of believers and smiling. We only had one late arrival — our sweet Deb Grimes walked quietly downstairs to join us during the Gospel reading.

As "Go in peace to love and serve the Lord" was spoken, the place came to life. Everyone pitched in to gather items into cars to head to the Knights of Columbus hall for the second day of the Conference. As we were packing things up, our neighbor Mark was unpacking items in his yard for a yard sale. Linda whispered to me, "Is he the one you've spoke about? The Jewish teacher?"

"Yes," I replied.

Off Linda went like a shot. She made a bee-line for Mark. She wanted him to know that there were Catholics out there that loved and revered God's chosen people. What an ambassador for Christ she was that day!

By the time we arrived at the K of C hall, Mary Dow was already there and hard at work. Mary was a whirlwind all unto herself!

Mary greeted us with orders. "The kitchen's all ready for you, Deb."

"Thanks! Can you help carry in breakfast cinnamon rolls that Katie made?"

"Sure!" Mary replied.

The Conference was a full-service of breakfast and lunch. Mark, Deb, Katie, Mary and I took on the brunt of expenses for the weekend events. Mark helped carry in the meats and crock pots of food before he left for work. We were so glad he would be off in time to help pack everything up at the end of the afternoon.

As we were preparing for the start of the Saturday conference, Hurricane Irma was barreling down on Cudjoe Key in Key West as a category 4 with 130 mph sustained winds. All through the day, prayers from our group went out for the safety of everyone in its path.

Our dear sister-in-Christ, Katie Yocum volunteered to stay at our home and make dinner for the 12 people we were expecting to come back with us for the evening meal. Boy was I glad she did!

On Saturday morning, Fr. David's talk started on time. In six short hours, he covered not only his life and conversion, but the church history of Mary, various popes and how, from his view, it all intermingled together.

Fr. David went from chasing drugs and women to chasing God. He never looked back, except to tell others of his transformation from a person of despair to a person of hope.

During Fr. David's afternoon talk, I had to excuse myself, went home and picked up some items we needed to finish his portion of the conference. Because of this, I learned second-hand, snippets of what he spoke about.

In the afternoon, Fr David spoke of the Biblical explanation of the Virgin Mary's role in Salvation history and her relationship to the Catholic Church. He related many of the messages Mary gave in personal revelations to various visionaries, including Sister Lucy at Fatima.

The messages the Virgin Mary gave were warnings to pray and prepare for the battles against the Church. But not only the church as a whole, families and marriage were under attack — and that was just the beginning.

Everything Fr. David led up to by the end of his talk, brought him to his reason for contacting Mark and me, and the Learys. We were receiving the same messages he was — and confirming what he was hearing. These are the days of the coming of the Lord. Prepare yourselves . . . pray, pray and pray!

By the end of the "official" conference, people gave generously to his cause and I even managed to sell a few books, too.

The Gospel of Mark, Part II
(That evening)

By 4:30 mass was over and we started the arduous journey of packing it all up to take it back to our home. What we didn't know was, our journey together was just getting started.

And what God had planned, as usual, was much higher than our plans....

Katie greeted us as we arrived. "Come in! Come in! Dinner is ready!" She cried.

"Oh, you jewel! What a help you are!" I responded.

Beef stew and chicken & dumplings awaited us. Along with the left-overs from the conference, a feast loomed before us.

Everyone gathered around for the evening prayer of thanksgiving. We bowed our heads anticipating "amen!" and a meal together. As soon as the quick prayer was over, chatter rang among our guests as they helped themselves to dinner. Our visitors represented almost 1,000 miles worth of a gathering. From New York to St. Louis, to Wisconsin, people came and sat, once again, in our home. And we were mighty glad to get to know them, each and every one. The count was twenty-something by then, not the 12 we'd planned for. But the meal held out—with left overs. A remnant was seated in our home: they came from Catholic, Christian and denominational churches—all coming together to hear the good news of the Gospel of Jesus Christ.

I remember one family in particular. They were from West St. Louis. They wanted so badly to understand the times we were living in. They had asked their local priest over and over for help. He refused to answer their questions. But there in our home, their questions were answered and they were not turned away.

As dinner wound down, our kitchen crew went to work. Linda, Carol, Deb, Katie, Mary and Mark started the clean-up. As we worked together in our kitchen, conversation of a higher sort was going on in the sunroom.

When we joined the folks in our sunroom to settle in and consider the deep things of God and how they related to the times we were living in, questions were being passed around. A couple of our people had met our neighbor.

They whispered, "Do you think he will come and talk to us?"

They asked Mark, "Would you mind to please go over and ask your neighbor if he would come over for just a bit?"

Now, our neighbor had just had as big of a day as we. He is a one-man army when it comes to yard sales. And it was almost 9 p.m.

While we were busy discussing whether our Mark (Peyron) should even go over there to bother him, he had already slipped out of our house and across the street. He stood on our friend's porch and knocked. Mark came to the door wearing shorts.

"Hi, Mark." He said.

Mark Peyron just smiled and replied, "They're waiting. Won't you come and speak for a little while?"

Mark nodded his head and asked my husband to wait for a few minutes while he changed. Then they walked back across the street and into our home. He promised he would speak to our group for a few minutes....

Mark told our neighbor he would be speaking in front of Christians of all denominations, including a Roman Catholic priest and two female pastors. They were all of great faith.

As the men walked into our home, whispers began.

"He's here! He's here!"

When they walked into our sunroom, Katie jumped up and ran out of the room. While they positioned themselves for the talk to begin, Katie was back in an instant dropping paper and pen in my lap.

Katie whispered to me, "You'll need these..."

"Thank you" was in my eyes. And once again*, this is where the Gospel of Jesus Christ met the Gospel of Mark...

Mark started the conversation with, "I'm sure you've heard about and seen the "Great American Eclipse" that just happened. It will cross America again in seven years — April 18, 2024."

*See MI-V, "The Gospel of Mark" for the 1st story.

46

Heads nodded including his. Then Mark's conversation went in a different direction.

"The Jews in Israel are very secular—especially in Tel Aviv. They are non-practicing in faith and modern in their thinking. The Jewish faith has 613 commandments. We also have dietary laws. There are things that are permissible and things to eat that are beneficial. So there are differences in traditions of people with the same heritage.

The Zionist Jews who are democrats are not for Donald Trump — even though Trump is for Israel and Jerusalem as their Capitol city. They are more pro-democratic party than they are pro-Israel."

Mark asked for a glass of water and went on with his ten-minute talk that turned into an hour and ten minutes.

"I would like to teach about some of our Jewish celebrations and our words associated with them. *Awe* - means to stand in awe of God. *Rosh* means "heard." And *ha' shamah* means year. *Rosh Hashannah* - the Feast of Trumpets.

A *shofar* is a horn blown to call people to synagogue, or at a time of warfare. A horn taken from a ram, gazelle, or antelope was used as musical instrument. The term was taken from Abraham: When Abraham took Isaac up the mountain to sacrifice him as the Lord commanded, the angel stopped him from taking the boy's life. The horns of the ram tangled in the thicket was sacrificed instead. Its horns became the first shofars. Jews believe one was

47

for the earth, and the other is in Heaven. It will be blown when Jesus comes back a second time."

As understanding hit our crowd, "Ohhh's" and "ahhhhs" went up in the room. Mark went on.

"Many major events have occurred on Jewish Feast days. As of the 21st century, we are in the 6,000th day of creation."

Just like watching a well-told movie, our group was translated from Corydon, Indiana to Israel, and back and forth as in a time continuum. You bet no one moved from their seats. We buckled in and scarcely breathed.

"In Jerusalem there is a small building with ancient writings in it. It is practicing this mystic writing where men learn how to make creative power without God. They are using creative power wrongly.

"Since the 1960's, science has been trying to figure the age of the universe. Socrates taught there was no beginning to the universe. Years later, scientists found there was a signature 'echo' of a bang. This beginning is where the Bible and science come together to prove the words, 'In the beginning...'"

Polite clapping went up with approval of Mark's message. He went on.

"There was a Jewish professor of cosmology of nuclear science at MIT who proved a theory that took 13 billion years down to 6,000 years. In the vastness of creation, the Talmud — our oral tradition — looked at created man and the planets in the sky. With all this knowledge and the Hubble telescope, they can see the edge of the universe—where time started, the edge."

I was taking so many notes so fast I thought my hand might cramp up!

More ohhhs and ahhhhs swept through the room with each bit of information Mark shared with our group.

"Were you aware the angels look at man in awe about our faith in God? Angels don't understand choice. (For the rebellion had been preplanned upon.) There really are sons of satan."

Mark paused and people gasped as the realization of the fight between good and evil settled into their minds.

I had personally felt that way too. *(As explained in the beginning of book VI, "Warn Those Who Will Listen," in story, "The Death of the Soul.")* Long ago, I spoke to one of these on the phone. The angel that guards me cried out, *"Hang up the phone! You are speaking to the damned! Hang up the phone! You are still speaking to one of the damned!"*

Mark continued, "Over in Europe, Muslim refugees rape and murder. They worship a god of war. Which can be traced all the way back to King Og, who was 19 feet tall.

"Our world is prophetic without even knowing it. There will be a millennia reign. The 'Days of Awe' are near the Feast of Trumpets, in 2017 the 21st-23rd of September. 3,650 years ago there was an exodus out of Egypt. Moses had an almond staff — it looked like a golden wood."

As we "travelled" back and forth in time, hearing how it all related together, Mark spoke on many more topics. Including Planet X and how it is associated with "Wormwood." The state of Arizona and Project Lucifer — how scientists since 1984 have been watching a brown dwarf star with the appearance of 'inbound wings' with its trajectory toward Earth.

"There will be a lot of magnetic upheaval to the core of the earth. A few years ago, radiation had gone up 12% and coming from within, not without. It has risen 24% in the last two years. This has been a great rise of concern with people on our planet."

Mark also believes Planet X is between the sun and the earth. It is at least 9 million miles away. It will not be a direct hit, but he thinks the earth will run through its tail, causing plagues from toxic elements. "If the poles change — it could cause a flash freeze on parts of our planet."

Mark has come to the conclusion that the Illuminati is a real entity. It does have to do with satan. And they are trying to pick presidents and world leaders—as they have been for centuries.

"Donald Trump is a phenomenon. The enemies of America are fighting him all the way."

Mark cautioned each household to have enough food and water to last at least one month in our homes. He reminded us that the Year of Jubilee would end at the end of September, 2017.

Then we went on a history lesson. "The Ottoman Empire ruled what they called "Palestine" for 400 years. From 1517 to 1917 until the end of World War I. the English took, what would later become the land of Israel, without a shot. They created the Balfour Declaration giving the land back to its rightful owners. All the way to 1917, it was desolate land – barren. But once the Jewish people began coming back to their homeland, the land itself began to flourish. Now the whole world is focused on Israel. The Dead Sea has so many healthful minerals. They make soaps, bath salts, facial and body creams from the salt and Dead Sea soil.

In Israel, every day they are finding in that region, gold, oil and natural gas. As the middle-east runs out of its resources (water, oil, money) watch, in 20 years, all those rich countries and families will be Bedouins again. Tent dwellers."

The whole room took on a collective sigh as Mark took a drink, only to start up another amazing discourse once again.

"September 23, 2017, Revelation 12:1-3 lines up – Jupiter [the star of the Messiah, the star of the King and called the "King Planet"] has been for the last nine months in the womb of constellation Virgo — the virgin. It is another sign in the heavens."✶

✶ *The planets Jupiter, Mercury, Mars, Venus and stars aligned to make 12 stars around the head of the Virgin constellation, with our Sun on her shoulder and the Moon was indeed under her feet – just as described in the book of Revelation.*

John and Mark commented on how they felt President Trump could be the last president to come against an antichrist. We all wondered if we would be here to see the end of days or rapture out — when the Holy Spirit is removed from the earth. John had previously seen in a vision the "taking up" at the end when the comet hits earth.

Mark once again took us to historical and biblical perspective. "In India, everything's a god. And that is why they are starving to death. Food all around them that they can't eat.

"Goliath was a Nephilim giant. He had poor vision and couldn't move quickly. His blood line was cursed. How do we know this? The Hebrews were still working with bronze weapons — swords. Goliath's sword was made of refined steel. It was a real weapon of war. It was the technology of the fallen angels brought down to earth."

Mark chuckled for a moment and shared an observation. "Americans treat 'crazy' as bad. Other nations in Europe and Africa call them, 'touched by God.'"

He moved on to other subjects.

"King David was a prophet, King, Priest. Jesus was a prophet, King, and Priest, too." (Yes, Mark believes Jesus, Yeshua, is the Son of God.)

"I know, all you hear about on American television is how much Muslims hate Americans. And they do. But Muslims hate Hindu's the worst. If they could, they would fight each other first."

Mark and John carried on a discussion as to who they thought the antichrist was and if he was on the earth now. As they put their information together, each asking the other more questions, we all began to wonder if indeed there was validity to their assumptions.

I tell you here and now, I believed them. We all believed that all those in that sunroom would live to see the antichrist make an appearance on the world stage. And I am grateful to say, we believe he is not an American nor associated with America. (Thank God!) John believes the antichrist is a man named [L.M.] who lives in London, England. He is of both Muslim *and* Jewish heritage.

Time flew by and before we knew it, we had kept our patient young neighbor way past his agreed time limit. People clapped and thanked him for his time and Mark walked him back to his home. Meanwhile, we were all so excited over our new-found information, sleep was far from us for hours to come.

John, Carol, Linda, Mark and I ended the evening saying prayers for Florida, as Irma had sustained winds of 130 mph over Key West. We prayed for the "giant of giants" to turn from the major portion of the state. We knew, millions of people were praying with us for lives to be spared.

Sunday
(September 10th, 2017)

By Sunday morning, after mass and a big, hearty breakfast, Fr. David was leaving. I was right on his heels questioning him like I was his big sister.

"Do you have the brownies I made you? Do you have enough medical supplies, Father? Did you forget anything? Let us know when you arrive at your next destination safely. Good bye, now! Good bye!"

Mark and I waved him down the street until out of sight.

God bless the man! Before he left, he heard my confession. I felt, for the first time in my life, like I was finally, really absolved of all of my past sins. It was my time. Fr. David shared and shared his gifts of seeing into another child of God's heart and listening to the Lord on how to heal their wounds with comfort and spirit. I am sure I was walking on air....

Around 11 a.m., Pastors Sherry and Linda from Wisconsin came by for an hour to visit with our remaining guests. Of course, healing was in the air. Pastor Sherry had sorrows in her heart. God gave John words of knowledge and comfort particularly for her which lifted her heart.

By noon, our Linda from New York was packed and ready to go. We had already shared tears of sorrow. The Lord had told her at mass, she would never see us again. We gave each other parting gifts. Since she had been to Walt Disney World officially two more times than we had, I gave her one of our best Walt Disney bath towels with Winnie the Pooh on it. She absolutely loved it! She also had a gift for me as well. A beautiful blue ceramic coffee mug made by Abbey Press. Written on it was, "Lord, make me an instrument of thy Peace." And on the top of it, "Blessed are the Peacemakers, for they will be called children of God." Matthew 5:9

By mid-afternoon, all our guests were gone and on the road except for John and Carol Leary. We thought we were on the quiet side of the weekend with plenty of leftovers. Ha, ha!

At 3 p.m. Mark, myself, John and Carol were in prayer once again for the state of Florida. We kept track of our Thomas Andrew and his family.

To make me and everyone else happy, Andy and family stayed two days at a Disney hotel to 'weather-out' the storms. They arrived at their destination as Irma made a second landfall off Marco Island at 3:35 p.m., heading north, bringing a storm surge and heavy rain to Sarasota and Tampa Bay. It had completely skirted a head-on collision with the middle of the state, where our son and his family were at Walt Disney World.

(WDW built every one of their hotels to stand up against high-category hurricanes. When severe weather is headed Florida's way,

Disney cancels reservations for those outside their state, gives patrons their money back, and opens their doors to Florida residents who are in direct-harm's way. They also open up their rooms for those that work there-like our son and his family. Disney Corporation is a fine example of an American company taking care of everyone that crosses into their World.)

We considered all of that good news, an answer to our prayers.

By the time we were ready to serve dinner, more friends showed up in our driveway. More people to feed from the leftover leftovers. But I tell you, every time I looked into our pots and pans on the stove, the more food there seemed to be. And wouldn't you know it, we just happened to be serving one of Fr. Mike Olsen's favorite meals.

Of course we were.

Fr. Mike came in carrying his oxygen tank behind him. His wife, Patti, came in carrying everything else. We welcomed them with open arms.

Fr. Mike started the conversation.

"I'm sorry we couldn't come to your conference, but we are here now! Is it alright if we crash your party?"

I replied, "Absolutely! You all are always welcome in our home."

Mark introduced the Olsens to the Learys. Greetings were exchanged and our new guests got to know our friends over dinner.

During the evening, Fr. Mike was asked to sit in the middle of our group for prayer. We prayed for the healing of his lungs. Although we did not see his healing in the natural that evening, Mike did feel good enough after being prayed for, to stay long into the evening and shared stories of God's wonder in all our lives.

What a way to end a conference...

Monday Morning Disappointment, Really?

(September 11, 2017)

By Monday morning, Irma had been downgraded to a tropical storm. Half of Florida's residents were without power and many airlines were having to cancel flights there, as well as all over the east coast...including the plane our friends were due to catch that evening. This led to a very interesting discussion over the phone...

"What? What?! What do you mean our flight is cancelled? We are going to New York - Rochester, not Florida!!"

It had hit the fan for our friends.

It seemed all flights on the eastern seaboard were being rerouted or cancelled. Thank God, John and Carol were still at our home and not stuck in an airport terminal sleeping in an uncomfortable chair—which I did remind our unhappy, stranded-for-a-day guests. I put on my best face possible and went into the conversation with joy. I hoped, at the time, my plan worked to ease their hearts.

"Oh boy! You get to stay for my world-famous pot pie I'm making for dinner! Katie and Nick will be over, too. She never misses when I make a pot pie." Well, at least it sounded like something to look forward to.

We also found a mass and adoration going on in Corydon. While there, I got to watch John in action-speaking with the Lord-on paper. It was incredible. It was as if all the rest of the world had fallen away from him as he wrote notes on what our Lord God was sharing with him. I marveled at what I saw.

Later that afternoon when we arrived home from church, Carol wanted to help cook. And John found we needed help with a new computer set up—which we did—dire help, because we sure didn't know what we were doing. And he did a marvelous job. It looked like we still needed each other after all. And because they weren't leaving until the next afternoon, Mark was off from work and able to go to the airport with me for hugs and prayers good bye. We sure hope, one day again, we get to see them.

On the way back home from the Louisville airport, there was no time to waste. Mark and I had but two short weeks to get ready to go and see our children — you know, the ones down in Florida that had no power?

We were taking our first two-week vacation since 13 years before when we harnessed up for *"Wagons West!"* moving the Schwarz' from Jeffersonville to Washington state. *(We had taken our friends from England, David and Dianna Gething along for that ride. Please see* Miraculous Interventions II *for the crazy antics we got ourselves into!)*

We were completely sure, this time, nothing could go wrong. After all, you would think, one time of unusual circumstances popping up over an extended trip would have taught us a lesson. But, no...we tempted fate once again and planned one week in Florida at Disney with our children and one week in Tennessee at a Christian conference. Why, we had even been invited to set up at their fall festival with my books and Katie's soaps.

We had reserved a suite for the Yocum's and us in a hotel in Tennessee for the five-day event. We were sure we were ready for anything...

...well, almost anything....

Miss Linda

(September 14, 2017)
(Recollection of a 2014 story)

As life wound down, and prepared to wind back up for our two-week trip, I heard from Linda, our new friend from New England. She had a story to tell me. And I promised her, I would tell you...

Linda is a faith-filled Roman Catholic. She says, part of her life's mission is to go on retreats. Back in 2014, while on a retreat to Montreal, Canada, she met a certain priest, Fr. Pat, and a lady. They asked Linda if she would like to have breakfast with them.

While they were in line to pay for their breakfast, another priest was there. His name was Fr. Alexis. When Linda went to pay for her meal to get into the restaurant, a ticket popped up from *inside* her wallet.

Fr. Alexis said to her, with a smile, "God will provide."

They all sat together.

During the meal, Fr. Alexis turned to Fr. Pat and said, "When these events are over, you will still be here, and part of a new priestly ministry."

Fr. Pat didn't believe him.

Later in the day, Fr. Alexis and Linda went on a bus tour. They ended up eating lunch together. Linda offered to pay for their meal and went up to the register with cash in her hands.

"Your meal was already paid for."

Once again, the good priest replied, "God provides."

Linda and Fr. Alexis agreed to meet for dinner later that evening at Madonna House. Yes, she would need tickets to get in. And once again, tickets popped up from her wallet.

"Okay, Fr. Alexis, say it." Linda said to the priest.

With a laugh, he said, "God provides."

Linda never had to use her money for meals during that whole trip.

Another priest named Fr. Eric joined them for dinner. Fr. Alexis started the conversation.

"There will be a great earthquake." That got everyone's attention. He went on to talk of the devil's final battle.

The good priest was asked of his fellow travelers, "Where did you come from, Fr. Alexis?" for, by then, they realized they were not listening to an ordinary conversation.

Fr. Alexis spoke of how he had been moved out of various communities. He had seen many evils—and complained. The 'higher-ups' were not happy with him. Finally, while assigned in Florida, and while taking food to the poor, he told a friend, "They are not happy with what I do. Something might happen to me. The 'higher-ups' don't like the poor..."

The Holy Spirit showed him who to speak to. And he had been sent to Montreal and Quebec to warn people.

The next morning, true to form, another ticket popped up in Linda's wallet. It was Fr. Alexis' last breakfast with Linda.

Fr. Alexis said, "It is time for me to leave."

He tried once again to speak to Fr. Pat about the word of knowledge he had given him. Fr. Pat still did not believe him. At that point, Fr. Alexis slammed his hand down on the table.

"Pay attention!" He shouted. "This is important! You have to know this!" Again, Fr. Alexis referred to a book called *Devil's Final Battle.* He offered Fr. Pat his phone number. He did not want to take it. Then, Fr. Alexis asked for Linda's phone number.

Right away, Linda said, "Sure!"

Fr. Alexis' last words to her there were, "If something happens to me...."

When he walked outside, there was a man waiting with a car for him. They had never met before. It was the way it always was for him. Fr. Alexis' life was a total walk with God.

Update: Christmastime 2016

Linda spoke with Fr. Alexis shortly before Christmas. She did not share with me their conversation. But she did share this...

After New Year's, Linda had not heard from Fr. Alexis. She called down to St. Petersburg.

"I'd like to speak to Fr. Alexis please."

"He died."

"Ohhh...."

As she hung up her phone, she breathed, "But there was nothing wrong with him...."

A Last Note

Before he passed away, Fr. Alexis sent Linda his book (*Devil's Final Battle.*)

A Much Needed Vacation
(September 26- October 7th)

My Lord! How can I tell you how weary I was? We were? Mark and I needed a break. He was cast head-long into this "prophecy" which had been trailing after me for months.

We had prayed day and night against a nuclear attack on American soil. I had seen open visions of a bright light early in the morning with an exact time of 8:15 a.m. I had cried.

I heard from several different sources that the same vision had been seen by other people too. One a priest and the other an ordinary lady such as myself.

If only I had indeed told all the right people. And dear God, let that letter I had sent to our president through a visiting pastor, have made it to its goal. The warning had stood in my heart, all through September and October. I felt, if we made it past fall without an incident, then I would have indeed told the right person.

For months, we had taken every waking daylight hour to work landscape jobs and painting jobs in order to afford the two weeks off. Because of the visions, we wanted to go and see our children in Florida – especially then. It was that important to us.

In our eyes, it all fell together for the second two week vacation we'd ever taken. Surely, we thought, it would go much better than the last one.

Don't count your "betters" before they arrive...

"Frick frack! Frick frack!" I yelled. (And that is the closest interpretation you will get from me, thanks for asking.)

"What's wrong with you!?" Mark asked. Frustration had settled in before we had even got out of our driveway!

I had everything packed — which was monumental for a two-week stay away from home. Plus we had books packed for the conference during the second week of our trip. And that money was to be used to go to a conference at the end of October down in Louisiana. Not quite like "robbing Peter to pay Paul."

"I can't get the rental car started!" I cried. Literally cried.

"Calm down!" Mark shouted. "You are too wound up! Give me the keys!"

Shaking, I handed over the keys. For Mark, the car purred to life. Sigh. I was in mid-repentance to the Lord when Mark spoke again.

"Let's go honey. You are sure you have everything? For the whole journey?"

I meekly said, "Yes." but I was feeling pretty humbled.

Off we went. Our first day, we travelled to Tennessee to spend the night. Then the next day, a long 12-hour trip to arrive at Andy and Sam's. We were to spend one night with them, and for the next five nights we would be staying on property at Disney. We had even arranged for Andy and his family to have the room next to us for 3 days too. The last of our savings well spent.

The weather was calm all the way down. Yet, we saw remnants of Irma's damage the farther south we traveled. High stacks of palm tree leaves and debris were on every corner. We knew that by prayer alone, Florida had "dodged a bullet."

We were greeted outside our car as we arrived at their new apartment home. Lily had Sophia on her hip and Matthew was bouncing all around. Papaw and Grammy had come to visit!!! All three children were shouting, "Grammy, Papaw! Grammy, Papaw!!"

As soon as Mark had stopped the car we fairly jumped out and ran to them with open arms. Those sweet dolls have trained us well. More subdued than the children, but still happy to see us, Andy and Samantha met us with smiles and hugs. Sweet kisses were exchanged. At last, we were all theirs as they showed us around their new apartment. Baby Sophia had to show us "right now, Grammy!" — her new big-girl bed.

Dinnertime came and Andy asked us if we had seen the newest Disney movie — which we hadn't had the chance. In just a few minutes he had it up on their television screen. In my mind, I flew back in time as I remembered running home from the grocery store on Friday evenings, shouting for all to hear, "I've got it!

I've got the newest Disney flick, you guys! Movie night! Family night!"

We spent most of the next day with them, then headed into our resort reservation late that afternoon. Mark and I had decided, months before we left home for this trip, we wanted to be good to our son and his family. They had been so good to us through the years, we thought giving back to them in the form of a mini-vacation with us would be a nice way to repay their kindness. We paid for them to join us for the weekend – Friday through Sunday – our hotel rooms next to each other. And our grandkids could stay with us.

For the first time, in 20 visits over 40 years, standing at the check-in reservation desk, I asked a question I had never once asked before.

"What you got going around here?" I didn't realize the words had come out of my mouth until I heard them.

The woman eyed me for a full minute before answering me.

"We have the flu – Influenza – from people coming in from other countries. Hospitals and clinics are full of it. Be careful."

I replied, "Thanks for the warning...."

Mark and I checked in and took the entirety of our week-long luggage to our rooms. Then we went to the boat dock to take a ride in to Disney Springs to meet our children for dinner. Pizza was on the menu. We'd promised we would buy all their meals during our time together. Their money was no good.

Dreaming in Disney
(September 28, 2017)
(5:30 a.m.)

After a nice meal and walk around together, the kids went home to pack for their weekend with us. And we went back to our resort to rest for the busy weekend ahead. Even as urgent as the message had been that had brought us there, I went to sleep at ease, to finally rest...

My "Telling" Time

I went to sleep and opened my eyes. I saw hell. It was all around me. I was in hell but not a part of it. It was as if I was falling down a long, black hole, into the earth. I saw what I thought was coal glistening and flash firing in the walls of the cavern as I fell endlessly downward. I soon found I was being directed where to go.

In this vision/dream, I reached a large cavern, bigger than I could take all in. I did not stop there. There was a second cave, farther down into the depths of hell, off to the side, as if it had been dug deeper into the very pit of hell. I was aware of a stench, horrors, sorrow and despair; but they were not a part of me nor of my experience.

I realized I was with an angel and it brought me great comfort. We slowed our progress and came to a room lit by a single candle. There was a table with no chairs — for there is no comfort in hell.

On the table were plans of a sort. Much like you would see in a situation war room. Out of the darkness to gather around the table, came hideous demons dressed in general's uniforms. The most ugly of all— ha' satan —lucifer himself — walked up to the table and spoke.

"Get ready. I am starting the war soon." His raspy voice seethed with venom giving me chills up and down my spine.

As soon as he spoke, I was back in our bedroom wide awake, heart pounding.

Immediately I was given revelation. I felt in my spirit, "Imminent! Days! Weeks!" And I felt I knew why. The devil was trying to start a war before the second coming of Jesus Christ. Satan thought the body of Christ couldn't stop his plans without the Man-Jesus physically on the earth. Satan was once again trying to usurp God.

I gasped. "What do you want me to do?!"

In my spirit, the reply came quick. **"Pray the Lord's Prayer! God's will. For the devil can't win against God's will!"**

I shook my husband awake.

"Mark! Get up! I've seen hell! Been to hell! I've heard the devil's plans! We have to pray! Get your Bible please!"

The urgency in my voice got Mark's attention. He quickly grabbed his Bible and we went to Ephesians 6:10-16 - the armor of God, as a sword and a shield.

At sundown of that very day, was Yom Kippur - the Day of Atonement.

I believed it.

I found out later, Katie Yocum was also up at 5:30 that morning praying. Sleep finally came back to her at 6:30.

Birds of a feather prayed together 900 miles apart!

40 Years Later
(1977-2017)
(Age 19-59)

On Friday the 29th, Mark and I decided to go to the Wilderness Lodge for lunch and a visit. While there, I received a text.

"Where are you?"

I replied, "At the Wilderness Lodge having lunch. Where are you?"

We hadn't expected the children until late afternoon.

Reply from Samantha, "At your hotel. Surprise!"

It was barely 1 p.m.

Replied again, "Lol! We will be right there!"

"Mark! The kids are already at our resort! They are surprising us! Whew hew! Let's go!"

Thankfully we had driven our car so we arrived quickly back to Port Orleans Riverside. Thank goodness for MapQuest!

We ran into the main resort's lobby looking for our family to check them in.

"Hey you guys! It is so good to see you all, hours early!"

Samantha laughed, "We were here early to surprise you, and it looks like we were the ones surprised!"

Hugs and kisses once more. We checked them in, paid their tab and took them to their room next to ours. Andy wouldn't be joining us until he got off that evening. The rest of us had a dinner reservation at our resort's restaurant. I had brought two new dresses to wear for nicer meals. Well, sweet Samantha had not brought a good dress. I looked at the two of them and picked one out for her. Well, it looked so nice on her I told her she could keep it. We took a picture of her in it and sent it to Andy. He loved it.

At the restaurant, as we walked to our table, above us were the inner-workings of a mast and ship. Papaw and Matthew loved looking around! Two-year-old Sophia had a blast with crayons and coloring pages. Miss Lily sat there elegantly alongside her mother, Sam. Dinner was Bayou cuisine!

After a wonderful meal and a happy-birthday-celebration dessert, (the next day was my 59th birthday) we walked all along the shops, the pools and took a look around, while waiting for Andy to arrive. We brought our grandchildren's luggage over to our room and Sam set up the play pen for Sophie to sleep in. It was her thing to do when away from home.

The next morning we started the day off early with our customary trip to Kona Café' for breakfast, – and for Papaw to get his yearly supply of Kona Coffee to take home with us.

We were celebrating my 59th birthday in Epcot. Andy was able to get off early that afternoon to join us for dinner in "Mexico."

Earlier in the day, I saw out of the corner of my eye, Mark getting water from a water fountain.

I screamed, "NO!!! What are you doing?!"

Mark looked surprised, then laughed. "I'm thirsty. I want water."

"NO!" I shouted with emphasis. "Don't you remember what the lady said at the front desk? There's a bad flu going around! Germs live in water fountains! Go buy your water!" I was frantic.

"You're exaggerating!" Mark exclaimed. "I'm not getting sick. And I'm not paying for water." To prove his point, he took a big gulp right in front of me.

I was sad to no end. Even with all my nurses training, all my words of knowledge, all he had seen, Mark rarely believed me...I had a bad feeling....

The rest of the day went very well and before we knew it, we looked up and saw Andy walking toward us.

"Hi Daddy!" Shouted the kids.

"Hi, Son." Mark hugged Andy.

"Hi everyone!" Andy smiled, then stopped. He sighed and said, "I'm starving!"

"Come on son, I'll buy you lunch!" I volunteered.

"Thanks, Mom."

We took off for a lunch area to get him some portion of a meal before our dinner in two hours. We brought Sophia with us. I was overjoyed to watch the exchange between an almost-3-year-old and her father. Their playfulness, their talk and laughter made my

59th birthday even more special. Soon, we rejoined the rest of our group.

For the next couple of hours, we looked around, rode a few rides and then headed for our dinner in the Mexican pavilion. It was a restaurant that in all our 20 visits, we had never noticed. Really didn't know it was there. You enter on land but are seated with glass walls all around you looking straight out over the water. There were large wooden beams on the ceiling, with earth tones on the walls and floors. It was subdued ambiance.

Our host seated us and took our drink and dinner requests. Since none of us had ever eaten there, we had no idea how large the meal portions would be. Oh my! I thought we would need another table to put it all on!

In the middle of the meal, Andy said, "Momma, come here and open your present."

"Present? You got me a present?!"

He was all smiles, "Sam and I went and picked it out this morning." Andy paused and asked, "You don't have any Disney jewelry, do you, Mom?"

"No, son, I don't." Unwrapping as fast as I could, I opened the small box. There sat a beautiful heart-shaped necklace. Faux diamonds were all around a picture of Mickey Mouse. It was just the right present for a jeweler's wife.

"Oh! It's lovely!" I cried.

I walked right over and gave Andy and Sam hugs and kisses, the children too. I showed it to Mark.

"Oh, please honey! Put it on me! Put it on me!"

Pictures were taken, smiles all around, happy laughter abounded.

As we headed back to our cars that evening, a storm was brewing. We all hurried back to our rooms.

Sunday was their last day in the hotel with us. They packed up their bags to take home with them. The time had gone by too fast. I knew Sam had to take Andy to work that morning. The rest of the gang would join us in Magic Kingdom. And she was late getting back. And the clothes I'd seen Andy wear out the door seemed awfully casual to go to work in. Hmmmm....

Mark and I stayed near the dock waiting for Sam and the kids to arrive. Finally, around the corner they came. And Andy was pushing Sophia's stroller!

"Surprise! Surprise!" They called out.

"Andy! Andy!" I was so happy I was in tears.

"I took the day off, Mom. Happy Birthday!"

Well, I started blubbering and crying. I kissed him over and over. I really meant something to our youngest.

Laughing in his usual way, Andy cried out, "Enough, Momma! Enough!"

He waved me away. Sam smiled.

As we had so many times in his life, there we were, once again, walking around Magic

Kingdom, riding rides and watching shows. But now, instead of Mark and me leading the way, it was Andy and Sam who took over the helm.

We really hadn't planned dinner. We thought Sam and the kids wouldn't be with us and Andy would be at work. Around 3, we started looking up reservation times. "Rainforest Café, Rainforest Café" started rolling over in my mind.

"Hey, you guys. What do you think about Rainforest Café?" I asked. We were all in agreement. You couldn't beat the burgers in that place. Off we trekked to another Disney destination.

As we walked into the Rainforest Café, Sophia's eyes lit up. She was captivated by the animatronic animals as they came to life.

After we were seated around our table – amid human and non-human chatter, – the seven of us ordered burgers and fixin's. Our time together was neither over yet, nor cut short. We were still together, sharing laughter and a meal. Our hearts were all set on one another, after all, as far as we knew, the world was still at peace.

We walked around after dinner until it was time for the kids to head for their home. We kissed 'bye' and promised we'd see them for dinner at their house the next night.

We would spend Monday day, exploring Animal Kingdom Lodge just the two of us. We slept in that morning and lazied until time for our lunch date at the Lodge. We tried out unique meals and went out afterwards to see the animals that roamed the premises.

Dinner was at their home. The girls, Sam and her friend, Kiera were making dinner for everyone. Everyone included all seven of the children, them, us and their husbands. Wow what a group! The ladies handled it like clockwork. We thought that was the last time we would see them for that trip. After all, we were leaving early Tuesday morning for Tennessee, right?

103.1° What?!

(Tuesday, October 3, 2017)

Mark and I hadn't been to breakfast yet. We were too busy packing. I would pack a stack of luggage and Mark would take it to our car. I packed another stack of luggage and he took it to our car. The third stack of luggage was all small bags and blankets that would go in our backseat.

Mark came back into our resort room just as I was finishing up.

"All's ready honey." I said, "We can go down to breakfast now."

As I was talking, and turned from him, Mark got back in our bed, shoes and all, grabbed the covers, pulled them up to his neck and preceded to shake the bed.

I cried out, "What is wrong with you?!"

Mark stammered, "I don't know. I hurt all over and I'm so cold!"

Our bag with medical supplies, including a thermometer, was still in our room. I touched Mark's forehead. He was hot!!

"Oh my!"

I dug out the thermometer and put it in his mouth.

Mark was saying, "I hurt all over...," as I put it under his tongue.

"It sounds like you have caught the flu." I went straight into nursing mode. I took his blood pressure and his oxygen stats – all normal. His temperature was 101.2°.

"I don't understand it. You don't shake like this unless you are over 102. You are nowhere close to it. This doesn't make sense. Maybe my thermometer isn't working. I'll call Sam."

Mark laid in the bed, miserable while I got our daughter-in-law, the ex-emergency room nurse, on the phone.

"Samantha? This is Momma. Something's wrong with Mark. He is showing a fever of 101.2, but he is shaking the bed like crazy! I think my thermometer is on the fritz. Do you have a thermometer?"

Samantha put on her nursing hat right away. "Yes I do, Mom. Come on over. I'll be waiting at the door."

"I'll be driving sweetheart. It may take a little extra time. I don't know the way like Mark does. Even with directions on our google maps."

"I'll pray for you, Momma."

"Thank you, sweet doll. See you in a bit. We are checking out and getting Mark a bit of breakfast down as fast as I can."

I practically carried Mark to our car and bundled him up in our extra blankets. I drove us over to the main building at Port Orleans, where we were to check out and grab breakfast. I knew Mark would need medicine as soon as we got to Sam's. He would also need something on his stomach, whether he liked it or not. I walked Mark in and sat him down next to the fireplace.

I checked us out and ran and got us each small plates of breakfast. Mark could barely walk. He legs were cramping up in pain.

"You need to eat a little something honey. You are going to have to take medicine to bring your temperature down."

Try as he could, Mark could only get a few bites down.

We walked slowly back to our car, and I bundled him up once again. I put in the kids' address on my phone and off we went to their home. I could feel an emergency room visit coming on...so much for Tennessee that day.

When we arrived at Sam and Andy's, Samantha was already at the door — waiting with a thermometer in her hand ready to go. She was all nurse.

"Open your mouth, Dad. I already called Andy. He is aware of the situation." Boy, she was on it!

Sam hustled us over to the couch. Then she read Mark's temperature.

"103.1°. Dad, you've got to be seen right away."

Samantha dug around through their cabinets for acetaminophen, handing him 1,000 milligrams.

"Take these right away. I am calling and making you an appointment right now. Mom, I'm sending the link to the directions to your phone."

Boy that girl was on it! Within minutes, the "situation" was handled.

"Go now, Mom. I'll keep Andy informed."

"Thank you sweetheart!"

Weakly, from on the couch, Mark said, "Do you think this is necessary?"

Sam and I just looked at him with our jaws dropped. He nodded his head and gave us no more fight. I walked him to the car.

Sam called out from her doorway, "Call me when you know anything!"

"I will!" I promised.

Four miles never seemed so far away.

As we walked in, I said to Mark, "I'll fill out the paperwork for you, honey. Sit down. I'll be right over there."

I approached the reception desk.

"Thank you for seeing us right away. We are here on vacation to see our children when Mark woke up sick this morning."

"You are out of town visitors?" The young man inquired. Two nurses looked at each other. "Do you have any health insurance?"

"No, sir. No, ma'am," I said looking at them across the desk.

They looked at each other again.

Did I ever tell you I can read nurse language? "What's wrong?" I asked.

"There's a $500 charge for out of town."

"Oh no..."

I quickly gave my own credentials in the nursing field and asked if there was anything they could do about the cost. We put our heads together.

"Well," they started. "You say you are here visiting your son? So, it's a Florida address we could use, especially if you pay your whole bill today?"

Smiles were on their faces.

"How much would it save us?" I asked.

"Almost $200." They said with a grin.

I called Sam to make sure it was okay with them, and it was. Instant part-time Florida residents we became. Thank God!

Shortly after that, another nurse called Mark back to his room. They took his temperature. Still high at 102.9. They left with a report for the doctor on-call. He came in shortly with an update. While the kindly, elderly gentleman examined Mark, he gave out orders.

"600 milligrams ibuprofen now. Culture for the flu. And get him a blanket."

All was done in an orderly manner. Mark and I remarked about the serenity that seemed over the urgent care center. How peaceful it seemed.

Mark had felt compelled to pray for a young man with a broken collar bone in the waiting room and for the attending physician that saw him. The doctor was so touched by Mark's prayer, he held his hand and smiled. He told Mark he did not know how close he had come to the actual prayer on the man's heart.

"You don't leave until your temperature starts to come down. Then go to the pharmacy nearby and get your prescriptions filled. Get rest and lots of liquids." Doctor's orders.

His diagnosis: the Influenza of 1917.

Oh boy.

I started myself on Silver Shield right away.

It was late in the afternoon when I called Sam with an update. She had good suggestions for us.

"Mom, you can't drive all the way to Tennessee or anywhere with Dad that sick. I'm calling Andy. I think we know where to send you. It's only four hours away."

Of course Sam was right. The couple gave us information to their favorite hotel to stay at on the road just on the other side of the Georgia border. I made our reservation. And I called our reservation in Tennessee for the suite we had reserved and let them know what was going on. They were very understanding. The desk clerk said they would hold our room for us. Please take it easy on the road. I sure did.

Before we left Altamonte Springs, I picked up Mark's medications, some lunch and made sure he had his first dose down before 50 miles out. I drove three more hours and made it out of Florida and started looking for our exit. We arrived shortly after dark.

I checked us in to a beautiful hotel and room. To our blessing, there was a restaurant right across the street. We walked over to eat, with Mark in his jacket and hoodie pulled up around him. He ordered hot tea. I shoveled food and his medication down him for a second time that day.

The next morning we slept in until Mark felt he could travel another five hours to get to the Tennessee border—our next stop. It did not look like a good start to our week-long conference and Fall Festival scheduled for Saturday a.m. Katie and Nick Yocum were supposed to join us on Thursday for the conference and fall festival on Saturday. How was I going to tell them our plans were rapidly changing?

We arrived at church that evening with a very rough-looking Mark Peyron. One of our favorite people greeted us at the door. She knew immediately how sick he was. That's when she started shouting, "Oh no! We have already had that flu in these halls. We like to never got rid of it! Go and buy your DVD's of the conference, and go back to your hotel and rest. Maybe you can come by Saturday for the Festival. Go home!"

And we did just that. On the way back to our hotel, we stopped at the grocers. Our suite had come complete with a full kitchen, living room, separate bedroom and bathroom. Home away from home.

Over the next two days, Douglass Inn fixed breakfast, I fixed lunch and dinner. We stayed in our room, only moving from bedroom to living room to watch a little television and eat meals in the kitchen.

While there, we would go into our praying time together. It was during that time that Mark saw a tsunami wave coming from the ground itself, not water. He also saw a big cloud over a city that was near water. Part of the cloud dropped down engulfing the city. But it wasn't violent. It was a very interesting vision.

I called Katie Wednesday evening and gave her an update on our situation. We were still registered for a booth at the church Fall Festival. I was sure I could sell all my books, and Katie her soap, to make money for our next planned trip to either Ohio or Louisiana at the end of October. And we were hoping to meet up with the man we had sent the letter with back in July, to find out the rest of our story.

Mark and I made the best of the situation with his temperature going down day by day. By Thursday afternoon, we heard from Katie again. We thought for sure they were well on their way to Tennessee.

I heard a heavy sigh on the phone. "I have bad news."

I cried, "What's wrong?"

"Our van won't start. I've got Chris coming over later tonight to check it. But it doesn't sound good Deb."

I could hear tears in her voice—and mine.

If the Yocums couldn't arrive, I had very little to put out on a table. No decorations either. She was bringing everything. And I most certainly couldn't leave Mark for a full day to fend for himself. I have to admit, I cried like a baby.

By that evening, Chris confirmed the bad news about her van. It was going to cost $600 to fix. And the Yocums couldn't fix their van and come to Tennessee. They had to do one or the other. Sadly, I told them we would head home Friday morning. At the time, I didn't realize how early that day we were going to have to leave...

5 a.m. Friday

"What's wrong with me?! What's wrong with me?! My throat is so sore, I can't swallow or talk! And I have a fever!! How will I ever get us home?!" I shook Mark awake. Panic was in my eyes.

Mark cried out, "What's wrong?!"

I put his hand to my forehead and clutched my throat. I whispered.

"We have to leave now before I get worse, or I won't be able to get us home."

As we quickly packed up the car and checked out, I thought to myself, "Gosh, will I ever confirm my letter getting to the President?" At the time, it was the least of my worries.

I started out driving. But after a couple of hours in, I was feeling so poorly, I couldn't drive anymore. As sick as he was, Mark took over. I kept taking my Silver Shield to ward off what was taking over in my body.

By 9 a.m., we hit the Kentucky border, and I put in a call to our doctor's office.

I croaked out, "You guys! This is Debbie and Mark Peyron. Mark got real sick with Influenza while in Florida. It has taken us days to get this far. I woke up at 5 this morning with a horrible sore throat and temperature. Too weak to drive. Mark is driving. I need to see the doctor as soon as possible!"

"When can you be here? Can you make it by 11:30? We will hold your time for you! Get here but be safe!" What jewels they were! And we made it with ten minutes to spare. Thank God I did not have the flu. Our doctor figured I picked up a virus while at the hospital with Mark. He gave me medicine and sent us both home to rest.

Well, needless to say, Mark and I spent that whole weekend at home taking care of each other. Due to the extremely untimeliness of these events, we had no money to go to either Louisiana or Ohio for conference. But we still had a date for the last week of October to Michigan with Deb Grimes. Nothing was stopping that.

During our resting time the first weekend in October, Mark dreamed of money. He dreamed of three checks coming to us. Two have come true just as he saw. One was at Christmas time and one was during the summer. Both blessings that came down the pipe.

But that third check, the blank check, has yet to make its appearance. And where that money comes from, only God knows....

All That Could Go Wrong
(October 21, 2017)

It had only been two weeks since the poor ending of our last vacation. And there we were, packing to leave again. The good thing, we thought, was we didn't have to rent a vehicle. Deb Grimes had cars that were very capable of making the 7 hour trip to Michigan. *Or at least it sounded good on paper....*

Deb Grimes arrived right on time to pick us up for our long journey together. We were driving her husband's Nissan Altima for its good gas mileage. An Altima has a continuous transmission. We were told it doesn't shift gears. It has one continuous gear. We started off in good spirits.

Two hours later...
I spoke, "You know, Deb, I think your engine sounds funny. Are you sure it's supposed to sound like this?"

One hour later in Ohio...
While Deb was driving in Ohio, Mark asked, "Are the rpm's supposed to be that high?" (3,500 rpm's)
"Oh my!" Deb said.
"Slow down Deb. See if that helps."
Deb slowed down to 60 mph.

Within 15 minutes, at 55 mph, the engine was revving at 4,000 rpm's. We were looking for a place to stop at 8 at night on a Saturday evening.

But nothing we were going through took God by surprise.

"Get on our phone, honey! Find us somewhere!" Mark barked.

Deb was quietly praying for us.

"Get off at this next exit. There is an Auto Zone. Maybe they can help us trouble shoot the problem."

We limped the next three miles. Try as hard as he might, Mark could not get the cap off to check the transmission fluid. We walked inside and asked the manager for help. The young man at the cash register came out and tried to help us to no avail.

"Well, we can't go on," I said.

Mark replied, "We are going to have to find a rental car somewhere, and a Nissan dealer to take Deb's car to. We can't just leave it here."

"Mark's right," Deb said. "I'll call Dave (her husband) and tell him what's going on."

I joined the conversation, "I'll get on my phone and start looking to see what's open at almost 9 o'clock on a Saturday evening.

I thought, "Oh, boy. Lord, how are we gonna get out of this one almost 4½ hours from home?"

I sat down in a McDonald's and started looking for a "savior." Mark and Deb went back out to the car.

It took me only a few minutes of looking on my phone before I got really excited. I ran out the door hollering all the way to Deb's car. I was talking before I sat down and the door closed behind me.

"You won't believe it?!" I exclaimed.

"What?! What!?" They cried out together.

"One exit back, ten miles down, is the airport. And in the airport is an Enterprise. They are open until 10 p.m.!"

"Whee!" Deb cried out. "Now, all we need is a Nissan dealer."

"That's the icing on the cake!" I replied. "There is a Nissan dealer one mile from the airport!!"

We were all shouting how good God was all the ten miles down the road. We were sure, the car seemed a little better all the way there.

"Oh, thank Heavens you're still open!" I said as I approached the clerks. "We had some trouble." I explained our situation at 9:30 on a Saturday night, and asked to see any car they had available to offer.

At first, it was a small economy car. We weren't so much for being scrunched in. Then the next car was a super-luxury car for $340 to get us through Monday. None of us could afford that.

Finally, the nice lady at the counter said, "Wait a minute! Let me call to the other side of our lot. Maybe they have something over there that could fit you better."

"Thank you so much for trying for us. We really are regular clients. We appreciate all you can do for us."

One attendant told the other lot dealer of our plight and what we were hoping for. When she got off the phone, she said, "Yes, that will do just fine. Well, we have a brand new, 2018, with electric convert-to-gas car. It gets 50 mph and is $120 for the three days. How is that?"

Before she could get out "how is..." we were all praising God and shouting. We knew this was no coincidence. When they drove it over to us, it might as well have been a princess carriage.

"Woowww!" We all said in unison.

Mark and Deb finished all the paperwork and I packed the other car. Mark volunteered to drive the broken car to the dealership and I followed behind him.

We left Deb's car at the dealership with a note telling them we'd contact them again on Monday morning. It looked like our stay was going to be a little longer than we had expected.

At 10 p.m. at night, another two hours from our destiny, we found a place to eat dinner. People's tummies were getting seriously hungry.

It was past midnight before we arrived at our hotel. And we had a wakeup call for 8 a.m. to get ready for mass and fellowship. Our good start had fallen off-schedule.

Our One Day Stay...
(Sunday, October 22, 2017)

...ended up being two full days. We had to wait for the car on Monday. And after our hectic 16-hour day on Saturday, 6½ hours of sleep, we were glad for the extension of time. That morning, 'perky' was not our name.

7:30 a.m. - alarm went off.
"Ooohhhh....no...."

"It's not daylight yet. What's wrong here?"

Moaning ensued but we were all up. Each one of us had a half-hour to get ready. No time for a big breakfast. Once again, we were on the road in short order. We traveled almost an hour longer to a small church we had not seen before, to see a priest we had only heard whispers about. St. Stephen's parking lot was packed. We parked out in the "back forty."

"My gosh! How well-known is this priest?" I exclaimed.

We stood outside the church and took our pictures. We wanted evidence to take to friends back home that we had made it. When we walked in, people were lined up all the way to the entrance. But something was wrong – they were in the middle of the mass. I was sure we weren't late. Wait...what time was it?

I whispered to a man standing and holding a baby, "Excuse me, sir. What time is it here, please?"

"9:30." Chuckle. "What time did you think it was?"

We were an hour-and-a-half early for the 11 a.m. mass...and Father wasn't speaking until 1 in the afternoon. There was nowhere to go. All we could do was sit and wait at the church.

Meeting a Saint

(Sunday, October 22, 2017)

Normally, being somewhere an hour-an-a-half early would be considered good timing. No so much for us on lack of sleep and food. And it automatically made our three-hour stay at the church to six hours. And Deb Grimes was a diabetic.

The early-morning mass ended and people filed out. We took the opportunity to look for a place to sit. As I was looking in the back 1/3 of the church, Mark and Debbie literally hopped and bopped right up to the front pew, right side. They were all smiles. I sighed.

From the front to the back where I was, Deb hollered, "Remember Deb, I can't hear Father from back there. I have to read his lips."

I nodded my head at the two who were already nodding their heads at me as I walked up and joined them.

"Forgive me. I forget how large a deficit your hearing loss is. You cover it well."

I sat in the middle between Deb and Mark. We watched as the church got ready for services. Altar boys came bustling through; then the priest, who eyed us quizzically. I am sure he was wondering in his head, why strangers were sitting in his front row an hour early for mass.

Well, if we didn't do anything for obvious sake, we were then. Smile and nod, smile and nod. I have to admit saying to myself, *"Don't* *say this out loud...*Keep walking Father, nothing to see here....*" to a man in his own church. Keep my mouth shut, I wanted to still be there when the special priest arrives.*

Finally, church members, along with people coming to see the Canadian priest arrived. At least we didn't stick out like a sore thumb anymore.

Keep that sore thumb thingy in the back of your mind.

It was a conventional Catholic mass – very ornate with traditional bells ringing and kneeling at the altar for communion. All the things I remembered from my childhood before Vatican II. It was beautiful.

Father got up and gave the homily – he did a very nice job speaking on the Epistles and Gospel readings.

After mass, we had about an hour to wait before the visiting priest's talk was to begin. We got to know a few of the people sitting around us. And the Holy Spirit was very active talking to us!

First, it was me. I felt absolutely compelled, *"Write a letter to Father telling him your background and how you are getting the same messages he is at the same time!"*

"Okay! I'm on it!" I wrote for 45 minutes.

At the same time I was writing, I'd look over every once in a while and see my husband. He was just sitting there with the funniest smile on his face. At the time, I wondered what he was thinking about. Later, Mark told me he was in conversation with the Holy Spirit. And it went something like this:

"Do you see all these people?"

"Yes, Sir."

"Do you think any of them are judging people?"

"Maybe, yes."

"Are you judgmental?"

"Yes, Sir. There have been times in my life I have been."

"And what about the times Debbie has condemned the homosexual?"

"Yes, Sir."

"Stop judging! That is my job! You are to love people!"

"Yes, Sir!"

"Now, look at people differently."

"Yes, Sir!"

So as Mark was looking around at all the different people in church and in his life, he started to smile. And love them without borders. Hence the sweet, funny smile on his face.

While I finished the letter I had been assigned to write, I knew in the other front pew across from us, Father's entourage of people were sitting there quietly.

I walked over and approached Father's traveling brothers-in-Christ.

"Hello," I started simply. "I hear you've been told about me. I'm the author from Indiana."

The little group looked at each other and nodded their heads, "yes."

"I also know Father is very tired and can't meet with me, so I have written a letter to him. Holy Spirit is sending me the same messages at the same time he is getting messages. We are connected."

I held out the letter to the brother and he accepted it with a smile.

The lady next to him spoke. "Do you get messages from the Lord, too?"

"Yes, but it has nothing to do with my worthiness. It has to do with a deal my mom made with God when I was born."

"Ohhh."

"Quickly, I was born 3 pounds and 13 inches long. I was eleven weeks early. I came out with both lungs collapsed."

"Ooohhh!"

"On my third day the nuns came to tell my mother I would not live. I was blue and unresponsive. She had to prepare herself."

Sad faces were all around me. I went on.

"Well, my mother was a convert! She had great faith! Momma made a deal with God. She told him if He would let her keep me, she would dedicate me back to him. John Leary said she changed my destiny. At that exact moment, I became like Samuel, dedicated at birth back to God."

"Wowwww!"

"Since I was young, I have seen and heard angels, been sent on assignments to save homes from burning, babies from drowning, and many other instances like those throughout my life."

As they were starting to ask me questions, Father came out to the altar. I quickly excused myself and walked back to my seat to listen to the talk of a lifetime.

Since I do not have Father's permission to tell his story in this format, I will only give a couple of highlights of what he spoke about, and not his personal story nor his background.

The good Father spoke on how important it was to get out the message about love and family. Of all things, they were the most important to God. In these last days, we had to remember how to love unconditionally and bring our family and all we know into relationship with Christ Jesus. Father said the most important of everything God wanted us to have was a relationship with His Son, Jesus Christ.

He also talked about his love and reverence for Padre Pio, who was also a very gifted man of God. Father spoke on what a terrible situation the world was in, with hate, violence and broken families.

Father stressed how important "the family" is to God. The first mission of Mary and Joseph was to be a mom and dad. And if you lose your first mission, you can go crazy.

Well, I believed him.

Father said toward the end, love as Jesus loves. We are here to prepare the world for the coming of Christ. And yes, the dear man believes we are in the last days. Jesus is coming for His bride, soon.

While Father was giving his talk, a baby was crying in one of the pews. Well, that was like a magnet to him. He went running toward the family.

"Oh, Mamma! May I hold your baby?"

"Yes, Father!"

The baby boy instantly hushed. He looked at Father with wide eyes. Father just smiled at the sweet infant and used him as a teaching tool. The baby was falling asleep as Father gave him back to his parents. In seconds, the baby was crying. And Daddy had to walk him in the back of the church.

Toward two-thirds of Father's talk, he stopped and looked directly at Mark and me. Father came over and smiled at Mark and said, "What your name?"

"My name is Mark, Father." Mark said with a smile.

Father gently shook Mark's hand.

Then Father came over to me and smiled and said, "What your name?"

With the best smile I had, I said, "My name's Deborah, Father."

He took my hand and smiled at me. He patted my hand. Then just as quickly as he had stopped to speak to us, he went right back to his program.

Father ended his talk with an anointing and a blessing over the whole congregation. His exact words were, "You will receive more than you think." What a way to end a conference!

I found out much later from Carol Leary, that Father's stopping his sermon to acknowledge us, meant something. She had only seen him do it once in all their times together. She said Father must have seen something special about Mark and me to come over and shake our hands. It was a blessing for sure.

A Sore Thumb
(Same day, 4:30 p.m.)

As Father ended his talk with prayers over each person, some of the ladies got in line for the bathroom—including me. After all, there was no way we were missing one minute of his program.

When I walked back into the church, it was my full intention to go back over to Father's traveling companions and continue our discussion. Before I could get past my group, Mark reached out his arm and touched me.

He said, "We have to go now, Debbie needs to eat. She is ready to go."

Crestfallen, I looked at Deb, who just smiled and nodded her head "yes." I knew she had given up her only food—an apple—for me to make it all through the afternoon service. And Deb is a diabetic. I knew they were right. I sighed and said immediately, "Yes, of course." I gave one last look as we left the building, wondering, what would've been if I had stayed.

We walked the long trek back to our car all giddy about the talk and the man who gave it. We felt we had been part of something special. The way Father had stopped the services, took our hands, smiled and asked our names, I knew our life was on the right track.

Deb Grimes was all aglow too ...until we reached our car. We were all getting in, hadn't even closed our doors yet, when Debbie gasped!

"Oh! Oh! I've been stung by a bee!" She cried out.

Then I gasped, "Oh, no! Mark! Get it off her!"

Mark swatted it off her and out of the car. He pulled the stinger out of her thumb.

Although Debbie was shaking, she remembered the seminar we went to together on pain. She held her thumb tightly for 20 minutes. I administered ibuprofen and Benadryl. (I know, I'm a sad lot. But be prepared means something to me.)

By the time we arrived at a nice restaurant for dinner, we had all calmed down. Deb's pain was minimal.

Everyone had done their part. I could not pull the stinger out due to my allergy to bees. But Mark could. He saved the day for Deb. I came in as back-up support—as usual.

We had a lovely evening meal together. Our talk was still fascinating. But by the end of our meal, our short sleep and long day caught up with me. I needed to go to bed right then. Mark drove us back to our hotel as fast as he could. Believe me when I say I was the first one in pajamas!

The last thing I honestly remember, was Mark and Debbie still talking away...

Indian Chief Angel

(Monday, October 23, 2017)

It started out as an innocent request. All I wanted was a little cream for my coffee on the road home. While Mark and Deb packed us into the car before checkout, I went down to the front desk to request milk for my coffee...

"I'm sorry. If it is not out there past breakfast, we don't have any available." The patroness smiled.

"Ohhhh..."

Then she said, "Wait! There's our housekeeping manager. You can ask her."

"Thank you! Oh, ma'am! All I want is a little milk for my coffee on the road. Can you help me?" I asked.

The lady smiled congenially, "Well, let's go look over in the area and see if we can find any."

"Thank you for your help."

We went into the dining room and she looked all around. He co-workers had been thorough with their clean up. It was all put away.

"I'm sorry, I can't help you. You are just too late."

As she started to walk away, a man who also worked for the hotel—he was taking out the garbage—heard our conversation. He stepped into the situation. He called the housekeeping manager's name.

"I can help this lady. I'll take care of it. Come with me, please."

"Thank you very much, sir!"

He chuckled. "You can call me Chief. Everyone does."

I chuckled back. "Well, thank you Chief! God bless you."

"He has, in more ways than I can tell."

Chief took me up in the elevator to the second floor. We got off and walked over to a cubby hole where a refrigerator stood. Chief opened the door and there was a carton of milk. I held out my cup and he poured. I thanked Chief once again and tried to pay him. He wouldn't think of it. I argued that he went way beyond the call of duty. He replied he serves a God who goes way beyond His call of duty.

I showed him my cross and he showed me his cross hung around his neck. As he started to share part of his testimony with me I got excited.

I asked him, "Can you come and tell your story to my husband and sister?"

Chief replied, "No, I can't on company time." Then he smiled. "But...If you call the front desk and ask for help with your television, they will send me up and I will have time to talk with you."

"Okay! I'll call right now!"

I ran down to our room and opened the door shouting, "You guys! You won't believe who I just talked to! I am calling the front desk to have him come up here and talk to us."

I punched in the front desk number and waited for the receptionist to answer.

"Hello, front desk? Can you please send someone up to fix our television? The color is off...okay, thank you very much."

In just a few minutes, Chief was at our door. Mark asked him to come in. He waked in and started telling his story. Chief was once on the path of death and destruction. He used to be a drug addict, then he was caught and put in prison. While there, the Lord got a hold of him and he has walked with God ever since.

Well, praise the Lord, Chief believes in all the same things we do: Miracles never ceased; God never changes; Jesus is the Way, the Truth and the Life.

I offered him a book of mine.

Chief only faltered for a second, "I can't read."

He has tapes he listens to all the time. And remember, God found him.

We left at 11 a.m. sharp on Monday morning, heading back to pick up Deb's vehicle and drop off our rental. Funny, on the way home, we never had any trouble out of Dave's car after that.

It makes me wonder whether it was a big ordeal — to discourage us before we got to Michigan. Aren't we so very glad we didn't fall for it? We got to meet a saint and an angel out of the deal.

Amen and amen...

Sunday Evening after Dinner
(November 5, 2017)

I'm sure Carol and I are on the same time—eastern standard—I'm just not sure we're on the same "time clock." My bedtime is not her winding down time. And by the time we got off the phone, I was the one wound up...

The conversation started out well enough.

"Hi Deb! It's Carol. Do you have a minute? My daughter needs prayer."

"Of course I do! What's going on?" I asked.

"She had to go to the emergency room and we are asking for prayers."

"Sure we will remember her in our prayers this evening. What else is going on?" That's a loaded question for sure for anyone who knows Carol.

"I wanted you to know Father received your letter and he is going to read it."

"Oh! Good, thanks!"

"He has seen your books and knows some of your past. (I'm sure John spoke to him.) He too, feels time is short and Jesus is coming back soon. The devil knows his time is almost up."

I replied, "Many of us know and feel these same things. We are all on the same track. We confirm the word in each other."

Carol went on, "John is receiving the same messages too. The devil's time is up soon! And 2018 will be a hard, cold winter. *[Which it was.]* Get ready!"

Carol stopped for just a moment and said, "If an EMP comes, it will not only hurt America, but Canada too."

"I hadn't thought of that." I admitted.

"Remember how John had the vision of a man shooting the President?" Carol asked.

"Yes," I answered.

"Well, we got hold of someone to tell and the message was passed on."

"Thank God!"

The rest of our talk was riddled with stories of healings that had occurred down through the years. Carol said people are starving to hear the word and speak the truth and that miracles still happen today! Our supernatural life does not start when we cross through the veil, it starts here and now on the earth. We can absolutely have a supernatural life now.

And John and Carol still feel the "refuge time" is coming...soon. They now have a well put in. The man who drilled it said there were only two other people, not close to them, who had such soft, awesome water. John and Carol exclaimed, "Thank You, Lord!" He is always generous beyond measure.

Rebuke and Command
(November 10, 2017)

During a "high volume" speaking season with the Lord, He will send us significant messages. Thought I'd share a couple of them with you.

In a time of warfare, Mark received: **"Devil, retire to the Lake of Fire!"**
A command for sure!

When I heard President Trump say this [phrase], "Confidence of made in America," I heard in the Holy Spirit, "Confidence of Prayed in America."

Sometimes, God needs for you to be somewhere for a season during a season with a reason.

For example, the time I had a job for four weeks at a business 90 minutes away, one way in good weather. The reason I was there was to meet a lady and hear her story. It was about her husband and his out-of-body experience.

For another example, the time I worked for a "care clinic" just long enough to pray over a lady who was sick and she healed right there in their office. I was let go two weeks later.

And the time I worked in a doctor's office just long enough to give hope to a hopeless lady and her friend...and to buy a new car!!

What?! Keep reading...I'm getting ahead of the story...

You Want Me to Do What?!

(Second week of November, 2017)

"I'm sorry your children are having such a rough time." I sighed.

My best friend had come over to meet with Mark and me. When her heart hurts, our hearts hurt.

It seemed a couple of her girls were going through a really rough season. One of their husbands had been permanently disabled (right shoulder) at a work accident and subsequent unsuccessful surgery repair. At 30 years of age, with children and a wife to support, he was in a bad way. They needed to come home to regroup. This daughter went back to work.

Another daughter's husband had lost his job due to mismanagement of the upper management where he had worked. And they had three children. They would not come to live at my friend's home to regroup. They were going to stick it out on their own as long as possible. With little to hold onto, their "as long as possible" could be any day.

My friend was understandably forlorn about it all.

"With both of their husbands out of work, it's a hard time for both families. [The first daughter] agreed to move back home until they could get back on their feet. But, [the second daughter] is staying right where they are. She wants to get a job, but has no car. She will have to walk through the winter. I don't have enough resources to help everyone."

I looked over at Mark who seemed lost in sorrow and thought. We hugged our friend and prayed for her before our dinner began.

By the end of our evening together, I can't say our moods were much different. We just covered them with love. Mark and I fell asleep that night praying for their entire family.

Instructions came to me as I awoke the next morning.

"Give Erin your car so she may safely go back and forth to work. And give her half of what you have in the bank."

"You want us to do what?!" This was not the biggest thing the Lord had ever asked us to do, but it sure felt like it at the time.

"Tell Mark what I have told you."

"Can't you tell Mark?!" I didn't want to be in the middle of the firing line.

"I already have," responded the Lord of Lord and King of Kings. **"You are confirming it."**

Sigh. "Okay. I hope he doesn't shoot the messenger."

Complete silence. After all, I had already said yes.

Mark woke a few minutes later. I was pretty sure—at the time—I had stared him awake. I didn't say a word, at first. I didn't know how to start the conversation—a real first for me.

I finally said to him, "I have something to tell you about last night."

"What is it?" Mark asked innocently.

I drew in a breath, steadied myself, and outlined my defense in my head.

Then I went for it.

"When [my friend] was here last night, I felt so bad for Erin. I feel like we are supposed to give her our car."

Then, an incredible thing happened. If I hadn't been there to see it, I might not have believed it myself.

Mark brightened up, he almost beamed!

He replied quickly, "I felt that last night too! Did you feel it was a word from God?"

"Yes!" There was both of our confirmations. I went on with the rest of the message.

"And I heard something else too."

"What is it?"

I gulped. "Give them half of our savings."

Mark stopped for just a few seconds. He sighed and said, "Okay."

I asked, "Do you want to go on Thursday instead of prayer group, and take the car to them?"

Mark replied, "Sure. Call and make the arrangements."

The next morning I texted Erin. "We're coming by to see you tonight."

Erin replied, "Okay. See you then."

I am sure she was wondering what was up. Mark and I had never been to their apartment together for just a visit before. And I am also sure she cleaned all day long!

That night Mark and I arrived in two vehicles. One, an old truck without heat, and 260,000 miles, and the car we were giving away—along with half our savings.

As I got out of the car, I said, "Okay Lord, here we go."

Mark handed me the envelope with cash and I put it in my purse. We held hands as we walked up to greet Erin. Her family waited inside for us. We walked into their small apartment and were greeted by her husband, Chris. They were wonderful hosts with what they had to offer.

"Tea? Would you like some hot tea?" Erin offered. She was eager to share whatever they had. I thanked Erin and she made me a cup of tea with honey. Before we had a chance to sit down, Mark started speaking.

"Your mom came over and told us what was going on with you two. Erin, you can't go back to work without a vehicle."

Mark pulled out our car's registration papers from his pocket.

"We're here to give you our car," Mark said simply.

Well, the place went ape! Those two sweet kids couldn't believe we were giving them our only car. They cried. We cried. Erin and Chris had to sit down. Chris tried over and over to give us something in return. He ran around his house opening closets and doors to see if he had anything to offer. I ran after him crying.

"Stop it, stop it! If you give us something, this won't be a gift from us! It would just be an exchange, and that is not what we are here to do!"

Mark signed over our old, $650 vehicle with over 200,000 miles on it to children who thought it looked like Cinderella's carriage. He handed Erin the keys. That was when I handed her the envelope.

Mark spoke again, "This will help tide you over."

"Thank you, thank you."

"Thank God, it was He who sent us." I replied.

Erin walked us outside to come and take a closer look at her "new" car.

"Look!" She cried out, "We can all fit in it at once!" Erin saw the gift more clearly than we did.

"Now listen," I started, "Don't lose that envelope! There is $1,000 in it. Go back and get your credentials in pharmacy technician. Go back to work at your real job, career."

"Yes, ma'am! I'll work on it!" Erin promised.

Just as we had arrived, Mark and I held hands and drove home in a truck that was on borrowed time. We comforted ourselves with the thoughts of how, over the last year, Mark kept smelling new vehicles when we would drive places. We knew, something was coming down the pipe.

We hoped it would be soon. We were headed for winter without a heater.

A Gold Truck
Hunter to the Rescue
(Third week of November, 2017)

We showed up at Thanksgiving dinner in our 20+ year-old truck. Mark parked down the street. (Appearances, you know. No, his family never judged us by our vehicles-or lack thereof. Good folk, every one.) But Hunter Royal was known for keeping his precious family in very nice cars. It was I who hoped we weren't an eyesore to the neighborhood. It was our new reality.

While there, wonderful conversations were held with everyone old to young. One of the many, was a conversation with our brother-in-law Hunter, married to Mark's younger sister, Sandra. Hunter comes from a fine family and a father who taught him a good work ethic. This, and a sound education has paid off for this smart young man. Hunter has been blessed with opportunity, and money has always followed. He has taken excellent care of his wife and daughter.

During our conversation on a completely different topic, Hunter spoke of the possibility of selling his "old" truck.

I was quick on the draw.

"Does it have heat?" I asked.

Hunter chuckled. "Yes, it has heat. The air-conditioner could use a little help, but it's a good, solid truck. I was thinking about selling it for practically nothing."

I inquired further, "How many zeroes are in your 'practically nothing' brother?"

Hunter Royal laughed out loud, "$2,000.00"

Mark and I said together, at once, "We'll buy it!"

Mark went on, "I get my end of the year bonus in December. Can we buy it then?"

"Sure!"

We all shook hands. It was a done deal. Mark and I were sure, God was repaying us for our good deed a week ago.

And maybe, just maybe, the Good Lord was just getting started.

When Mark and I left the Royal home, we were so excited! We only had to endure a truck with no heat for a month, or so we thought. But God and the Royals had other plans.

By the middle of the next week, an advance check came in the mail for us for exactly $2,000.00. (And we paid that off three weeks later.) Hunter called and said to come get the truck. They were more concerned about us having reliable transportation, than them getting their money right away. Hunter and Sandy were very surprised when we showed up with cash in hand.

God had seen to all our needs.

Great Aunt Kate!
(End of November, 2017)

"Come on Katie!" I cried. "We're going out to dinner with our kids. We'll be back in time for Nick to pick you up."

"Well, I guess I could go," Katie reasoned.

"Awe, come on! You can play with baby Edward! He is so much fun!"

"Well, if you're going to play the 'baby' card, I'll go."

We met Ben, Amanda and baby at the Cracker Barrel. We all sat down to a good meal. Chatter rang throughout the busy pre-Christmas atmosphere. And that's when Katie got to shine. While busily talking at our end of the table, we heard from the other end, baby laughter. Real squeals! Loud and long laughter rang out to be heard in all the building. We looked down to see a thoroughly engaged Katie Yocum giving "knucks" to our 16-month-old grandson. Edward squealed and laughed to everyone's delight.

Katie laughed right along with him. She cried out, "Knucks, Edward!"

Edward held out his baby hand in a fist. Katie put her big hand next to his and made a blow-up, fizzle sound and animation with her hand.

Edward squealed with delight. The harder he laughed, the more it became contagious. First it was our table watching. Then we noticed others were watching too. As Edward's laughter traveled through the room and other sections, people stopped and smiled. Smiles lit the restaurant up as a baby's delight reminded us all of the real reason for Christmas...

*

Red and Gold at Christmas
(First two weeks of December, 2017)

I started a new job out of nowhere. The hours were great. The location was great. And the people were great. I would try as hard as I could. I thought surely the Lord had dropped opportunity into my lap once more. I wasn't finished or washed up. I would be working two jobs at a time! And I liked both jobs! What a help I would be to my husband!

Just days before, walking out of the grocery store, I looked down and saw myself in a nurse's uniform and shoes. I even made a comment to Mark.

"Honey, I think I'm going back into nursing. I just had a quick vision."

Without Mark missing a beat, he said, "Look for it, honey."

And I did.

December set up to be a very busy month. Mark and I would both be working six days a week. We had a gold "new to us" truck. We thought it kicked off our season of plenty just right. Even my godmother was in on the act. She had felt for a whole year, we would end the year better than we began it.

A Gift in Time Saves $12,000!
(Friday December 9th, 2017)

Over the next couple of weeks as paychecks started in from multiple jobs, Mark and I pondered—for the first time in our 20 years together—a car payment. Mark even looked on-line for a vehicle. He had car lots sending information to his phone. He had a nice gold truck, and Mark wanted his wife to have an equally nice car...and I never saw it coming.

"You want me to do what, after work?"

For the second time in a month, I was asking the same question.

Mark repeated his order. "I want you to go over to Heritage Ford and find us a car."

"Okay, I'll go look and see what I can find out." But I thought in my head, "But it's not looking so good at my new job, honey."

The day at the "new job" came and went quickly. Nursing can wear a body out! I left the hospital on a cold, windy afternoon and headed to Heritage Ford.

I pulled up to a parking space in Mark's beautiful gold truck. I walked into our local, Ford dealership. Heritage is a very nice, clean and spacious dealership. It is a wonderful, physical tribute to the hard work of James Hodge and his crew.

It was a Ford Dealership, but under another name before James Hodge bought it 32 years earlier in 1986, and renamed it "Heritage." (I believe the name "Heritage Ford" was inspired from above.)

Mr. Hodge had worked for Ford Motor Company for 15 years in Detroit as a field representative in auto parts service. But in his heart, he had aspired to run his own dealership. For a while, Mr. Hodge left Ford to work for a dealership to sharpen his skills about ownership. And to save and sacrifice for his 'dream come true.' Before James knew it, he was able to approach Ford and request his very own dealership.

"Why yes," Ford replied to James' request, "We have one available in Southern Indiana." And off the Hodge family went!

Over the years, James made it his personal goal and commitment to excellence to provide a valuable service to everyone who came through Heritage Ford's doors. James Hodge understood that his customers were his friends and neighbors—and he would treat them all just like that!

Over our years of living in Corydon, we watched them grow and expand. We always knew when America was doing well, as Heritage also did well. In 2008-2010, when the housing market/stock market threatened to take America down with it, Mark and I noticed the half-as-many cars on their lot. I cried and counted the months until things would look up again. I knew, when America came back, Heritage would too.

And boy, did they! As if intertwined together, as jobs came back in 2017 and the stock market rose, Heritage Ford seemed busier than ever! And that was where the Holy Spirit told my husband to send me.

Heritage Ford had two businesses under their title: New vehicles and used vehicles. As I walked through their doors on that cold, windy day, my hope was that we would qualify for a used vehicle of any kind. Anything beat nothing.

I was a real mess when I walked through their doorway. The wind had whipped my hair around, my uniform was dirty from a day's work. What a sight I was! And I confess right here and now, I knew nothing about cars. What had my husband been thinking? And that is how 22-year-old Cameron found me as he walked up to greet me.

"Hello! Can I help you?"

I opened the conversation with sheer honesty, "I, I, I'm not sure. I don't know. I think I'm here to buy a car. But I don't know beans about cars!"

The young, sandy-haired gentleman chuckled good-naturedly as he responded. "That's okay! I'll help you. Come sit over here and we will piece a car together for you."

"Thanks so much! I'm such a mess. Please forgive my appearance. It's so windy and I just got off work. My husband sent me over because we need a second car."

"You're just fine," Cameron waved away my anxiety. "Sit down here. I'll go get my computer and we'll pick a few cars for you to look at. Would you like anything to drink?"

"No, sir, thanks. I brought my water in with me."

Cameron and I sat across a table from each other. He pounded the keyboard looking diligently as information flashed across his screen. I sat in confusion, waiting for him to ask me questions.

"Okay," Cameron started, "What would you like in your car? What kind of style do you like? Name some things you've been thinking of."

"Well," I began, "a good engine would be nice—with some get up and go. And," I brightened, "my friend Katie Yocum has heated front seats. I really want heated front seats!" I sat smiling.

Cameron typed in, "Heated front seats. Got it."

We waited for the computer to spit out its answer. Within seconds we had our reply.

Cameron spoke, "Two on the lot have your requests. One is being test-driven now and the other is right out here. Let's go look at it."

We stood up, put our hats, gloves and coats on and walked right out the front door to a white car. It was the only color Mark and I agreed on that we didn't want. I sighed.

"Uh, no thanks. White is the only color we agreed on that we don't want. So sorry..." I said.

Back to the drawing board...uh... computer keyboard, we went.

Cameron looked at me and asked, "What did you think you were coming over here for?"

I made my confession, "A slightly used car. I don't think we can afford a brand new vehicle. In 20 years, this will be our first car payment."

I had just impressed our car salesman. "Wow...we don't see that much around here."

"I know," I replied. "We're a different duck. But we do have great credit!" I smiled.

The young man sat and pondered for a few minutes. And then he pondered some more! Then his face lit up with an idea!

"You know, we have here on this lot, a car that we use as a loaner or rental. It's less than two years old, it has heated seats and lots of nice extra packages." By then he was looking at it on-screen. "And it only has 13,000 miles!"

"How much?" I asked, sure it was way out of our ballpark.

"I think I can get it for you for a little over $15,000.00."

I dropped my jaw.

"Wow! Are you kidding me?!"

"No!" he cried. "Our 2018 rental has come in and we can sell this one now."

At that point I excused myself to go to their restroom. The minute I walked in there, I got on my phone. I looked up Kelly Blue Book to see how much the car was worth. I knew it was such an excellent deal, I could hardly believe it. I put in all the information Cameron had just told me and tried to get an answer on my screen, but it wouldn't show it. I walked out and back over to where Cameron was sitting.

"I need help!" I confessed.

Cameron looked up quizzically. The last thing he knew I was in the bathroom! What could go wrong there?!

"I tried to find out how much the car is actually worth, but I can't find it on Kelly!" I looked miserable.

But not Cameron, he brightened right up. "That's a great idea! Let's look it up!"

Well the truth of the matter was, it was such a great deal, it was hard to look up. We finally figured the car was worth almost $4,000.00 more than he was quoting to me. I felt in my heart, God had hidden the car just for us.

"Want to take it for a test drive?" Cameron asked.

"We can test drive it?" I asked. Boy am I green.

"Sure! Let's go!" Cameron nearly shouted.

Off he went to get the keys. When he came back and we were walking out the door, I asked, "What does it look like?"

"The color is Ruby Red."

"Ruby Red." I repeated. "You mean like for a jeweler's wife?"

We stopped and stared at each other.

He replied slowly, "Yeah."

Cameron and I walked across the lot and across the street. We arrived at the "practically brand new" car. I couldn't believe it. In all my wildest dreams, I never thought I'd own a Ruby-red Ford Fusion. I was looking for *ordinary,* and God was laying *extraordinary* at our feet. True to its name, it sparkled like a ruby.

All I could think to say was, "You drive."

Cameron got into the driver's seat, made sure I was buckled in and took off for the suburbs of Corydon. He was right, it rode and drove wonderfully, and had lots of pick up.

I asked him, "Do you know where Albin Jewelers is?"

Cameron replied, "I sure do! I do business there. Is that where your husband works?"

"Yes, Mark is their bench jeweler."

"I know that guy! Let's go show him a car!"

We arrived a few minutes later and walked in. Mark greeted us.

I said, "Hi honey! Do you have a minute to walk outside and look at a car with us?"

"Sure!" Mark replied.

As we walked out, I whispered, "Fifteen thousand. And it only has 13,000 miles." I nodded my head as Mark looked across the street at it.

All he could say was, "Woowww!" and smiled like he just found a diamond . . . uh, ruby.

"Come sit in it, honey," I suggested.

We all sat down in the car. Mark and I in front and Cameron in the back, ready to answer any questions we had.

After a few questions from Mark, he asked me, "What do you think?"

I replied, "I believe God saved this car just for us. It has waited for us. Just like our last car the Lord sent us."

Mark's mind was made up. "Go start the paperwork. I get off in twenty minutes. I'll see you over there."

"Well, Cameron," I smiled, "I guess you just sold a car today!"

We were all three all smiles.

"Great! You drive back, Debbie."

"Oh!"

I drove back very carefully.

We walked back into the dealership and Cameron asked me again if I would like some coffee. That time I said thank you. We managed to get half way through the paperwork when Mark came walking in. Yes, he had coffee too. They ran our numbers and came back with a yes from a bank in less than 20 minutes.

Their response to us was, "We don't get people like you in here every day."

Cameron said, "I feel like I've sold you the car you'll have the rest of your life..."

Just before we left the building and we were walking past the greeting desk, I saw a plaque sitting, facing the public. It was scripture. Heritage Ford had scripture presiding over their business. I jumped up and down with joy! Do you know, before that moment, Cameron had not noticed it?

It was long after dark when we left Heritage Ford. Cameron had agreed to come out and sit in our car and show us how everything worked. He spent almost an hour with us answering questions and sinking our phones with the computer. Mark gave him a tip for all the time we had taken up. We parted as friends.

I drove Mark over to his truck.

I said, "Now we don't have to rent a vehicle anymore when we travel!"

Mark and I drove both our vehicles home. We went on our first excursion to show off our new car. We went out to dinner and to see the Christmas lights over in Brandenburg, Kentucky. And I got to use the heated seats!

....

Special shout out of thanks to Bert Hodge, James' son for all the background information he shared with me for this story. Bert has a wonderful story to tell also, and a great faith walk. Maybe one day, with his permission, I'll tell his story too.

Peace, brother-in-Christ.

And thanks for your service to our country.

Ruby Red for a Jeweler's Wife
(December 13th, 2017)

Because of working two jobs at the time, I worked ten days straight. I finally had one day off, the 13th of December. Who could I go see and show our new car to that would be happy for us? Why, our oldest son, of course.

Text: Lunch?

Reply: Sorry, Mama. Not working long enough today for a lunch.

A few minutes later...

Text: Ok. Lol. Who do you know? Someone called in and now I work all day. Lunch is on. One o' clock okay?

Reply: See you at one!

I walked into the nursing home Ben worked in as a physical therapist assistant. All the patients and staff knew him.

"Ben Merk?"

"Yes, that's my son."

"Straight down the hall to the waiting area. He should show up running through there."

"Thanks."

Sure to what the receptionist said, it wasn't a few minutes before Ben went zooming by.

"Hi Mama!" Ben called out. "I'll just be a few minutes more."

"That's fine, son. I'll wait right here."

True to his word, a few minutes later, Ben appeared in coat and hat. He introduced me all the way down the hallway, heading toward the front door.

"This is my mama! This is my mama!"

One old gentleman replied, "She doesn't look old enough to be your mama!"

Sweet old people!

We walked out and Ben said, "Where's your car, Mama?"

I chuckled, "Here it is, son."

I told him the whole story in three minutes flat. He loved the car and thought we got a good deal. But he didn't buy me saying Dave Ramsey would approve of the small car payment.

Since Ben was on limited time, we went a few blocks away to grab a burger.

After a prayer, and we began to eat, Ben started conversation.

"Mama, God has laid something on my heart."

"What is it son?"

"I think I'm supposed to feed the hungry this Christmas."

Ben explained the promptings he had been feeling and how he had been to talk to his counselor at church about it. Something was up in the supernatural.

Ben asked, "Do you think I'm hearing from God?"

I replied, "Yes sir, I do. I'm sure it's the same voice I have been hearing since I was a little girl."

After listening for a few more minutes, I stuck my hand out toward Ben. Puzzled, he took my hand and we shook.

"I'm in." I said.

"What?" he asked.

"I'm in. Whatever you need, I'll do. As a matter of a fact, there was a great sale a few months back on turkeys. I think we have five turkeys and two hams. I'll cook three turkeys and both hams we have. How's that for a start to something you only have two weeks to put together?"

The child brightened like a candlestick!

"Mama! You're wonderful!"

"Can we put it on Facebook and ask for donations?" I asked.

"Yes! I'll make an event out of it!" Ben answered.

The wheels were already turning.

"I'm sure if I put out a call for help, people will provide," Ben reasoned.

I asked, "Do you know where it's going to be?"

Ben answered, "Yes ma'am. Jeffersonville. There's a homeless shelter there. I'll start setting up from this end. We can talk again later with updates soon. Thanks, Mama. I'm going to call it, Nerds Serving Birds. I figure if people can go out and drop $20 for a movie premiere, they can drop half that to feed people."

"I love the idea!" I cried.

Ben smiled so big, "I'm going to be a Jedi Knight!"

Of course he was. A "Jedi Knight" for Jesus.

When I arrived back home, I looked at my calendar. I saw I was not off that day and only one day off that week. I wondered when I would have time to cook. How would I get everything done I had just promised I would do?

I was sure Katie and Debbie would help me, as they always do. The closer it got to that week, I realized how much I was relying on their help to make three turkeys, two hams and 300—yes 300—cookies.

Again, I was just sure everything would go fine despite my lack of hours in the day ...after all, I was going to have help.

Surely not all of it would fall on just my shoulders at the last minute....

Have you not read any of my books to date . . . ?

Confirmation of a Sort
(December 16 and 17th, 2017)

Let's recap the last two books of the *Miraculous Interventions* series:

Miraculous Interventions V The Small, Still Voice and *Miraculous Interventions VI Warn Those Who Will Listen.*

The warning in the fall of 2017 was about a possible nuclear strike from North Korea, although the first warning came three years before with Pastor David Becker, culminating at the end of book V for me. The verification came at the end of writing that book. All of book VI was about the fight to tell someone who would listen and do something about it. After all remember the conversation that started it all...

[Me: "What?! What do you want me to do with this information?!"

Holy Spirit: "For this, you have to do something. You have to tell someone. Tell all who will listen to you."

Me: "Pray?! What can I pray?" (Because I was panicking, quickly.)

HS: "Yes, you can pray against it. Pray for duds. That they are to be duds."

Me: "Yes, Sir! Duds, duds, duds, duds, duds -- duds in Jesus name!"]

My hope against hope came in, as higher and higher sources came around at just the right time for me to send the information up the ladder.

God sent the first confirmation that my message had reached the intended audience from a pastor in a small church in New Albany, Indiana. His visiting pastor had a word of knowledge that was so specific, there was no escaping it.

"You sent a message with a man of importance to a man of great importance. God wants you to know it got there."

I was sure when I went to Tennessee for a conference, I would get a second confirmation from their people there. Yet unfortunate occurrences struck. Mark was so ill (103.1 temperature) I was unable to leave his side and go to conference by myself. I thought I would have to be content with the word of knowledge from the evangelist.

And by the way, he prayed for blessings and protection over me and my family. We were going to need it.

Questions remained in my mind until the beginning of the third week of December (17th). I happened across an obscure eight minute you tube video. I have transcribed it here:

Title: North Korean defector says even a limited attack by US would trigger all-out war.

PBS News hour

Title of Article: Out of North Korea

This was viewed and transcribed from the airways and a public site on YouTube.

Transcribed here:

"As we reported earlier, President Trump departed today for a lengthy trip to Asia. At the top of the agenda will be coordinating pressure against North Korea. The regime of Kim Jong Un has made significant advances in its nuclear missile programs. The core message of the President's trip, 'We will not allow North Korea to have the capability to launch a nuclear-tipped missile that can hit the United States.'

So how does North Korea view its weapons programs and the Trump administration's approach?

We turned to former North Korean Diplomat Thae Yung Ho. He was once North Korea's Deputy Chief of Mission in London. He defected last year (2016) and now lives in South Korea."

"Mr. Thae, thank you very much for joining us. You were telling us that you led a pretty privileged life as a diplomat working for the North Korean government. Why did you defect?"

"It's a complexity of reasons for my defection. First of all, I did not agree with Kim Jung Un's desperate race of nuclear and ICBM programs which can finally make North Korea totally destroyed, and secondly because of my future of my sons. I thought as a father the best legacy I should leave for my sons is to let them free."

"We know this is a regime that takes defectors very seriously. Are you and your family safe?"

"At this moment I am not quite sure where they are. My family members and relatives are safe."

"The ones who are still in North Korea?"

"Yes. I have one sister and a brother in North Korea. And for propaganda work, last April, North Korea invited CNN team to have interview with my brother and my sister. In that interview, they cursed me a lot but at that moment I was really happy to see their faces again because I didn't imagine that I could see them again in my life after my defection."

"So as someone who worked in the diplomatic field for the North Korean government through many years, what can you tell us about the mindset of Kim Jung Un?"

"Kim Jung Un is not a madman. He is intelligent guy. But with a "muslis," (*unclear word*) mind. So the past five years of his stay in North Korea proved that he want to destroy anything in his way no matter whether it is a country or human being. He has persecuted hundreds of city leaders in North Korea in his five years including his family members like his uncle and his half-brother."

"His own half-brother. What do you understand to be his view of the United States? We have seen his nuclear build up. The missile build up. What is your sense of what he thinks he can accomplish when it comes to the United States?"

"He has kind of an illusion that if he acquires these nuclear weapons and ICBM he could be able to compel Washington to pull US troops out of South Korea. And once US troops leave South Korea then foreign investments would follow troops out of South Korea. And if that is the case, then the South Korean business also would leave. Then he can stabilize the whole South Korean system with his nuclear weapons."

"But we haven't seen that happen of course. And we are seeing is this administration, the Trump administration pursuing a very aggressive policy toward the North. What do you see as the effects of that on the North?"

"I think the Kim Jung Un has been very desperate to develop its ICBM and nuclear. And he even sent a lot of rhetorics, warnings and provocations of nuclear tests and ICBM tests. I think we should admit that some rhetorics by President Trump and the unpredictable character of President Trump actually worked to some extent to stop his desperate escalation of the conflict. For instance when Kim Jung Un want the possible test around Guam, the American

137

territory, then President Trump respond with fire and fury."

"That comment."

"Yes. And that kind of very strong response by President Trump actually stopped Kim Jung Un to have a test around Guam. That's why he changed the direction of ICBM from Guam to Pacific Ocean over the Japanese territory."

"So you are saying to some extent, that it's had a positive effect on the North?"

"Yes, I believe its so."

"And we know now from reporting that there are those in the Trump Administration who have put forward the notion of the possibility of a limited strike—an attack against the North in order to punish the North to keep it from developing its nuclear missile program, in the belief that that could be effective. How do you think the North would respond?

"I think even a limited strike like kind of strike by US can bring a full-scale conflict or war on Korean peninsula because all North Korean military have been trained to fire back anyway, if one of their army very small part of North Korea is attacked by the US. And given the fact more than ten million of South Korea population are living within one hundred range of tens of thousands of North Korea artilleries, missiles, I think it not, if that kind of immediate and automatic response from North Korea military can create huge human loss on South Korea side. And if that's the case, then I think America and South Korean forces may retaliate in full scale. Then that's why it will easily escalate into a full-scale war on Korean peninsula which would mean huge human sacrifice."

"Huge? Almost unthinkable?"

He nodded.

"You've also talked to us Mr. Theo about what you think would be effective. You are saying some of the tough talk from President Trump has been effective? But you've also said that there should be a better effort to communicate with the North? To reach out to the North? What do you mean by that?"

"I think we should engage in and even try a dialogue with Kim Jung Un and also we should engage to break the isolation of North Korean people. I think we can disseminate the more outside information to educate North Korean people so that we can help North Korean people to make a change."

"Fascinating to see where this is going to lead. Thae Yung Ho thank you so much for talking with us."

"Thank you very much for this opportunity."

Between January and August of this year (2017) 780 people escaped from North Korea. 57% were farmers and manual laborers.

Site: PBS News Hour
PBS New Hour You Tube video
PBS is a publically-funded American broadcaster.
This was taken from the common airwaves making it public knowledge.
Used with general permission.
(Verbiage transcribed as exactly as possible.)

To me, in my heart, this was the verification I—we—had done all the right things. From the Indiana pastor who put it out over the airwaves to get everyone praying, to my doctor who believed me, to our local law enforcement official who took a copy of my letter and two books! To the pastor who we believed took my letter to the President of the United States. Every one of us had a piece to help with in this. Not to mention all those I'd had praying, family members included.

From over four years ago with Pastor Becker, to this past summer with my friends from up north, and all in between, I believe we all had and have an integral part in the ongoing Saving of America.

And it's not over yet...

"I Quit."
(December 18, 2017)
(8:45 a.m.)

I couldn't take it anymore. It seemed as each week passed, I got worse and worse at my new job. It was as if God had closed my mind— for that season.

Yet my last day of work there, three days before, I had the opportunity to carry the Gospel of Jesus Christ forward with a couple of patients. I will relay only the good I saw come out of my time there. And I am sure, that office will forever think I am dumb as a box of rocks. If they ever read this, to them, I sincerely apologize for my lack of intelligence.

There were two ladies who had come in for a visit. One of them had a trying past with lots of regrets. I spoke only one minute of God's forgiveness and His plan of salvation; how it was hers for the asking. I wished them both better days and blessings.

As I was closing the door behind me, I heard one whispering, crying, "Who was that? Do you think she's an angel?"

And the other was a single lady waiting for a procedure. She looked very tired as I entered her room. As I was taking down her information, we spoke. She spoke of her fears and hopelessness about her perceived situation. Yet she wore a shirt with a faith slogan and picture. I responded quickly out loud, from my spirit.

"That's not what your shirt says to me. It says you are a woman of great faith. It takes courage to wear a shirt like that. There is more to you than you recognize."

Well, buddy, the lights went on in her head and shone out her eyes. She brightened up immediately.

She cried out, "I knew it! I knew it! God told me this morning he would send me an angel to encourage me! You are my angel! You are my angel!"

At that point, I got excited too!

"Do you know how special you are?! To be able to speak with God, you have to be a friend of God!"

"But I'm only a new Christian," she stammered.

"And the thief on the cross only acknowledged Jesus in his last twenty minutes of life..."

My gosh! I left her room crying.

When she came out after her appointment, it was as if she was a new woman—she practically beamed! She found me in the hallway and hugged me for a full minute. Then she was gone.

Three days later, so was I.

Tears and Regret
(December 18th, 9 a.m.)

My place of employment took it well. They said not everyone works out. Maybe something else would come along that would suit me better. I thanked her for her kindness.

I cried bitter tears all the way home. This was the first job in my life that I had not been able to do, despite my best efforts. I felt like such a failure. I had let that office down, I had let my family down. How could I ever be good at anything again? I was not wallowing in self-pity and drama, I was taking a full bath in it!

Once home, after a few more minutes of self-pity, I called my other boss at Harmony and Health and asked if I could have my old hours back. LaDonna came instantly to my rescue.

"Sure! I can put you on January's schedule," she said.

I am always grateful for her understanding.

Over breakfast, I listened to a young man speak on a word the Lord had given him that morning. "I will cover you where you lack." I felt his words were for me.

To prove his point, before the end of that afternoon, two people from Harmony and Health called me and said they heard I was coming back. Would I like some hours before my start date? They could both use a day off the week after Christmas. Because of that, I did not lose one day of pay. At the recognition of that fact, I cried tears of joy. Even though it was less pay an hour, I ended up with more hours a week so the pay evened out.

And remember I wondered how I would have the time to make all the food that week for Ben's feeding the poor program on the 23rd? (Even with the help I had coming...) I ended up having plenty of time after all...good thing too.

Ruby Red Sleigh

(December 18th-23rd, 2017)
(Monday afternoon, the 18th)

The Lord did not allow any of my time to be wasted. No time for grass to grow underneath my feet starting with the afternoon of the day I had quit. Calls already started coming in. I went from working every day for man to back to every day working for God.

Over the phone, Katie groaned, "My car radiator has to be fixed. Chris said he could fix it as early as tomorrow, but we have no place to fix it."

I replied, "I'll tell Mark when he comes home tonight to clean out our garage so we can get the front of your van in so Chris can fix it. I haven't had much time to fix anything for dinner for all of us..."

Katie responded, "Oh that'd be wonderful help Deb! I can cook and bring it over. Everyone can meet at your home. I'll be over early." Katie paused, "I'm sorry your job didn't work out for you. I know how much it meant to you to work in a doctor's office again."

"Me too," I sighed. "I sure hope God knows what He is doing."

"I'm sure everything will work out just fine. God's children don't go begging bread."

"Thanks for that timely reminder." I could always count on Katie Yocum.

True to my word, when Mark came home, he cleaned out our garage as best as he could.

Tuesday December 19th

I had our home all cleaned up before the crew of five arrived that afternoon and evening. Of course, that was Katie and Nick—the ones who needed help—and Chris, Eva and little Katie—the helpers.

Katie and Nick arrived first.

The first thing Katie said when she walked in our front door was, "Wow! Nice car!"

"Thanks," I responded. "It was a God event. I wonder if we will get to keep it."

Katie replied quickly, "If God brought it, He is not an Indian-giver."

"Yes, you are right," I smiled. "Thank you for that reminder."

I helped Katie with whatever she let me do for dinner preparation. Mark came home right on time. And how he loves to make an entrance.

"Katie! Nick!" He shouted with a smile and a hug.

In unison, we all three shout back, "Hi, Mark!!"

"Hi, honey!" As Mark got around to me with a kiss hello. "How was your day?"

"Better than yesterday," I responded, "Thanks for asking. How was yours?"

"It's the week of Christmas! It's crazy!" my husband, the bench jeweler, smiled as he responded.

We only had to wait a short while for the last family to arrive. Katie had planned a wonderful home-cooked meal for us. It felt just like family sitting together at our dining room table, heads bowed in prayer. Eva even brought us Christmas presents! It is one of her very favorite things to do—give to people. Eva and Chris have special hearts and spirits that have gone unmatched to date, in all the people I've yet to meet. With as little or as much as they have ever had, Eva would gladly give it all away to help another soul in need. I am very glad to have made their acquaintance.

After dinner, all the guys went out to fix the "van problem" and change their radiator out. All the women cleaned up our kitchen and dining room table.

Once the guys came back in, cards, games and fellowship were the next order of the evening. And after that, there was always time for a prayer meeting. Singing, praise reports and prayers were always on our agenda.

At the end of the evening, with laughter, and hugs given, we escorted all our dear ones to their vehicles and waved goodbye.

Midnight was fast approaching. I had an early-morning-duty at the hospital on Wednesday. My Godmother and best friend, Vicki Sampson, hadn't had such a speedy recovery from her knee surgery. She was still in the hospital, much to everyone's surprise—including her. Because of her extended stay, she needed a ride home. Was I available to help her?

"Why sure!" Two of my favorite words in the English language.

I could squeeze one more thing in to do while waiting to start cooking for an estimated 100 people that weekend. The turkeys were still thawing and the cookies weren't ready to bake yet. And my help were still on stand-by.

What else could happen?

Remember, this is me we're talking about....

Wednesday December 20th

Vicki Sampson was sure she would be going home by noon. She was to have her last physical therapy before lunch. I made sure I was there in time for it all.

I walked into Vicki's room with a greeting. "I'm so glad you are going home early. That way I can get you all settled in at your home before the boys arrive and take over for me." Now, please understand, her "boys" are 66, 63 and 58 years of age. But we have known each other a long time, and "ages" don't enter our hearts or conversations much.

Vicki said with a smile, "I know you will take good care of me, baby. You should make it home in time for dinner."

"Okay!"

Lunch came. Vicki insisted we split it—which we did. In the middle of our meal, a physical therapy assistant came by and picked her up for her last session. Vicki came back a short while later.

Vicki said, "I thought you might join us in therapy to see my progress."

I sighed, "I got stuck on the phone helping someone." It was par for my course.

Vicki finished her lunch and we sat and talked. When it was time for her "shows" to come on, we settled in to watch the afternoon away while waiting for her surgeon to make his appearance. While still waiting, Vicki's oldest son,

Michael and his wife, Susan showed up. Everyone was now wondering what the holdup was.

"No doctor to release you, yet?" Mike inquired as he walked in.

"Not yet," we sighed.

It was after 5 p.m. when I went out to the nurse's station and inquired about her surgeon's whereabouts.

"He only has one patient in this hospital. He will probably come here last," the day shift nurse replied.

I walked back to Vicki's room to report to our waiting crew. Vicki's dinner was on its way up. Darkness was falling.

Mike—my brother in my heart—asked me, "Hey Deb, you hungry?"

"Yeah," I replied.

"Susan you hungry?"

"No, I ate before you got home to pick me up. You all go on. I'll stay here with Vicki."

"Thank you," I replied. "We'll be back shortly. Thanks, Mike."

Michael and I talked all the way down to the basement lunch room. He is such a gentleman! My money was no good as long as there was a Sampson around. He bought me dinner. I have always had favor with Vicki's family, and I am glad of it. And they have always had favor with me. We are ready at a moment's notice to help each other out. We love every minute of it.

Mike and I sat down and prayed over our meal, and for Vicki too. We reminisced about our 43 plus year friendship, how to help Vicki and what would need to be done for her when she arrived home. We were still talking when we entered Vicki's room once more.

"Any signs of Doc?" we asked.

"Not yet."

It was close to 7:30 in the evening by then.

I began to prepare her for the thought of going home the next day. In the middle of my speech, at almost 8 p.m., in walked her doctor—with his five-year-old tagging along behind him. I almost stood up and clapped!

He is a very studious man, but not without his funny moments. He examined Vicki's surgical site, typed in his report on his computer and signed the 'okay' to dismiss her from care. Vicki Sampson could finally go home.

It was agreed Mike and Susan would take her home. I would look in on her the next week. Mike walked me to my car. Once again, "Nice car, Deb!" I drove off as we wished each other a Merry Christmas!

I still had one more stop to make before I arrived home myself, the grocery for last minute items to cook and bake with.

As tired as I was, I was sure glad I had help coming...

Thursday, December 21st

Sigh...as it turned out, all my help who was supposed to show up—couldn't. Katie had pneumonia (?!!!) and Deb had a terrible case of bronchitis. I was all on my own. And I'd had two very long days.

Well, I was in for another couple of long days. No time to complain, though. Just get up and go. Or did I say, "oohhh," as my "get up and go" had already got up and went before I had gotten out of my bed! And it wasn't even 8 a.m.

"300 cookies to bake–seven different kinds–okay, got it." I said to myself. I was pretty sure it was overload, but when was the last time a homeless shelter full of people was ever put first on the list of people to bake for with love?

During the middle of all the baking extravaganza, a thought formed in my head.

"Nerds feeding birds...and Ben and his people will be dressed as superheroes... hhmmm." I was pretty sure it was newsworthy. Why, wouldn't it be nice if they got a little press for all those good efforts?

During baking times, I started making calls to our local television stations. Two of them were interested in a good-news report for Christmas Eve. I gave each of them phone numbers and addresses where Ben could be found and where they would be in Jeffersonville.

Friday, December 22ⁿᵈ

Late night, early morning
Late night, early morning
Late night, early morning
Late night, early morning...I asked myself,
"How old am I?!" as I crawled out of bed that
morning. (59 and counting for nosy people.)

At early, "O-dark-thirty," Mark and I were already discussing hams and turkeys.

Mark offered, "I think you should cook the hams downstairs and the turkeys upstairs. That way you aren't lugging the heavier meats up and down the stairs."

"Deal." I was for it.

Twelve hours of continuous cooking did not fly by. I was exhausted and almost in tears when Mark walked through the door that evening. But boy did he look like "Mr. Wonderful" as he carried dinner in. He figured I had already done enough cooking for one day.

It was another late night and I still had to work early the next morning. And before I went to work, I had to travel across town to deliver a whole car-full of food to Ben's home.

I was up before dawn Saturday morning.

As I left out of our home and got on the road, I realized my Ruby-red car, had become a Ruby-Red sleigh just in time for Christmas.

Saturday, December 23rd
Jedi Knight Ben

I arrived at Ben and Amanda's by 9 that morning—food in tow. She and I packed it into her van, awaiting Ben's arrival from a store.

"He will be here in just a few minutes, if you would like to wait for him. He will want to see you."

By the time we were finished placing everything in her van, Ben drove up. When he got out and walked toward us, I had never been more proud.

"You are the handsomest Jedi Knight I have ever seen!"

"Thanks Mama!" He looked inside of their van and let out a slow whistle.

Ben hugged and kissed me and thanked me for everything I had done, all the people I had contacted who came through with help, all the cooking and donations we had given. It really was an army of love that had gathered together to help those less fortunate in our community. After all, Charlie Brown, isn't that what Christmas is all about?

Baby Jesus would have been proud.

Ben hollered as I was late leaving for work, "Take it easy on the curbs!"

"I will! I promised.

About the same time I was getting off work, Ben and his crew were wrapping up from the meals. That was when I received a phone call from him.

"How'd it go, pal?" I asked.

"It went great, Mama!"

Ben had several families show up from his church and helped serve. There had been so much food donated to feed those who showed up, not only did they have enough for lunch, but dinner as well. Praise the Lord!

Ben chuckled at the end of his recounting.

"Mama, did you call a television station to come and cover us?" He inquired of his slightly-elusive mama.

"Which one?" I asked innocently.

At that he laughed.

"I almost called them too, Mama. But I figured I would get through the first year and then see about calling them next year." Then he added, "But I am glad you did it this year."

I could hear him smiling over the phone.

"If it makes you feel any better, it wasn't entirely my idea. It dropped into my head like water." I added, "The Holy Spirit, you know."

"I'm sure it was, Mama, I'm sure it was."

It was channel 32 that came out and interviewed everyone. And they did a marvelous job showing the kindness of strangers in a season of love. And the volunteers' leader, was a Jedi Knight.

Channel 32 aired the clip three times. Thanks guys! Our hope – it would inspire others to get on board the Christmas train...

155

Sunday, December 24th

Ben, Amanda and Edward made a special trip to spend Christmas Eve at our home. They came out for an early-morning breakfast so they could visit with Mark before he left for work. Smells of cinnamon rolls, bacon, biscuits and gravy met the children as they came in carrying multiple packages for gift-giving later in the day.

Ben said, "It smells like a Marky Peyron kinda breakfast in here!"

"It sure is, son. Welcome and Merry Christmas!"

We gave thanks to our Heavenly Father and Jesus Christ for the meal and time to celebrate together. Discussion was lively as we caught up with each other's week activities.

All too soon, Mark was off to work and I was cleaning the kitchen, preparing a turkey (another turkey!) and making sure I had everything lined up for our afternoon brunch together. Middle son, David and his girlfriend Emily were coming over for the afternoon meal and gift exchange. It was our special time together, just for our immediate family of opening gifts and family pictures.

Dave and Em arrived in time for brunch before Mark got off work. They too, brought in copious amounts of presents to share their generosity with our family.

We went downstairs to start opening gifts, which we were still in the middle of when Mark came in. He brought a plate of food down with him as he joined us in all the comradery.

The highlight for all of us was watching sweet baby Edward opening his gifts. How he lit up at the sights and sounds of the firetruck Dave and Em gave him. It whirred and whistled and "sirened" all through our downstairs. Then, we pulled the blanket off the 3 ½ foot tall teddy bear that I had gotten him. My gosh, that baby squealed! That bear proudly sits in the reading corner of Edward's room, where mommy and daddy read him to sleep.

By the time we said our goodbyes, and our children left, we grabbed our overnight gear, the turkey, and headed to church with Mark's sister, Susan. We were 20 minutes late.

For the life of us, we could not find his sister. We sat in one of the back rows searching diligently for her. Finally, at communion, we walked right past her. We gave her pats and hugs. She was elated to see us. After mass, we headed to her home for the night.

Staying at Susan Peyron's is like staying at a resort. Her home is beautiful and spacious. Living room, family room the size of, well, our family room!

After we put everything away in the guest bedroom and put on our pajamas to relax, we joined Susan in her family room. She had snacks set out for us which we partook of. We talked until way-too-late in the evening, enjoying every minute. To us, it was the calm before the storm of people coming the next morning. Christmas and the day after zoomed by...

End of an Era
(Friday, December 29, 2017)

While at Harmony and Health a few days before Friday evening, in the space of two to three seconds, I saw a vision. (Sometimes, God will show me what is coming up next for me—in an instant.) I saw myself working with Mark in a jewelry store. I had on a dress and looked very professional, but comfortable. There were jewelry cases around; I saw the lighting, walls and felt the atmosphere around us. I wondered, at the time, what that meant. I figured I'd tell Mark that Friday evening at dinner. He beat me to the punch....

Mark walked in quietly from work. It was not his usual boisterous entrance. Almost immediately, I felt uneasy. He washed up for dinner as I made plates. After prayer, his dour mood continued. And I wasn't helping him, I was being a "snit" back. After a few minutes of banter, I apologized for adding to or putting him in a bad mood. His reply was it wasn't me.

"Then please tell me what is wrong?! I must've offended you because I can see it all over your face, and your mood."

Mark sighed, then he quietly spoke, "Albin's will be having a going out of business sale from February through this spring."

Mark's statement took my breath away. He let me in on all the details he knew, or thought he knew, at the time.

I cried silent tears as Mark told of the plans he and Lana were already making together. They figured they were destined to open their own store. Jim said he would stand-by to help them start up.

Finally, Mark said, "Honey, please stop crying. You're breaking my heart!"

"I can't help it, Mark. It's not just because I'm concerned about us."

I cried even harder. Mark got up and walked over to me and put his arms around me.

"What is it, babe?" He asked.

I sniffled and sniffled.

"It's the passing of an era. Albin's has been in Corydon for 70 years. Lana's been with Jim since she was 18 years old!"

I laughed.

"They get along like daughter and father. Sometimes that's feisty. But it all adds to the comradery of "the family." You've been with them or worked with them for almost 25 years. It's like a family break-up. You all kid around, care about each other."

I paused and thought. "I don't like it. I don't like this at all. Who will look after Jim? He is getting older. He will be home alone with Chloe (dog)....Mark, I'm scared..."

Shock settled in and I began to shake. Needless to say, it was an early evening. We went to bed and curled up together. I wanted to sleep through it all. We laid there and just looked at each other, whispering bedroom talk, wondering what the future would hold for us.

I thought of the new car I hadn't even made the first payment on. I hoped and prayed we would be able to keep it.

A Final Confirmation
(Long after I thought
I had finished this book!)

While Mary and I were editing this book, and I was waiting for page reviews to come back from New York, a package arrived.

In it, was a copy of a declassified report to, well, one of those "alphabet agencies" which I will not name. It was regarding the likelihood of an EMP threat from the North during the fall of 2017. And it was dated during the period of time which we were all getting alerts from heaven to pray like crazy against an attack! Even the date of September 30th was mentioned, just like in my dream!

This was the same month that North Korea detonated an H-Bomb under their mountain. (It caused a 6.0 earthquake, reportedly bringing down internal parts of the mountain, trapping and killing a hundred people.) And it released radioactive fallout over their area.

There was much more in this declassified report that was way beyond my ability to explain here. Suffice it to say - we got it right. The threats had been real and the warning came just in time.

Prayer and obedience do matter.

Epilogue

(December 31, 2017)

(Laughing)

Well, it appears, I have tried to say "the end" to the *Miraculous Interventions Series* with the last couple of books. I figured, "What else is there to say?" I wasn't going to share a warning, God said to share it. So I did. And I have told you what I know to date about it all. So when these last four books came to a close, I thought I was once again, "off the hook." But the Good Lord kept naming more.

If this tells me nothing else, it tells me that these books don't belong to me anymore – as if they ever had. They belong to all of us – to you, me, everyone involved. To John and Carol Leary who have joined our team – or we joined theirs! We are all on God's team together! Amen.

By the afternoon of the last day of the year 2017, I was deliriously happy we (the world) had made it through the fall mostly unscathed. No planet had knocked the earth out of its orbit (I believe because of prayer), and because of all the political efforts and faithful prayers, war was averted in the fall of 2017.

Oh! I just realized the planet-knocking-out-of-orbit story was not mentioned yet! I'll never forget my vision in early September 2017. Once again I was taken out of my body into deep space, just as I was when I was 38.

I looked out into the vastness of space and saw planet Earth. Off to the right, I saw another large planet headed for the same path Earth was on.

As I watched it getting closer and closer, I started shouting, "Stay your hand, Lord! Stay your hand!"

I panicked as I watched it from afar. It did not even slow down. I screamed, "Stay your hand, God!! Stay your hand!!"

With the next breath, all the darkness dissolved and I was back where I began.

Six weeks later, I found out the elusive planet which others too had been watching (called everything from "Nibiru" to "Wormwood") had become stalled, vapor-locked, behind the Sun. Its course had been "stayed."

It seemed to me, the Good Lord, in His infinite Wisdom, saved America. This shows He is as concerned about the saving of countries as He is the saving of souls. After all, He has a vested interest in all of it. From the smallest of details to the largest, He is in charge.

I have recently met a gentleman who thinks America is "toast." "Be prepared," he said. And I reminded him that "toast" is for another season, not yet here no matter how close it may be. He nodded in agreement.

We will live on to fight the good fight for another day, another season—no matter how short or long. But in my opinion, the last days or years are upon us.

And the surprise of surprises, Mark would be going into business during this new season. No rest for the weary. Because of it, I was sure my writing days were coming to a close. After all, how can you top averting a war? If even just for a season?

That's when the Whisper came, as always, out of nowhere, ***"Extraordinary Miracles, Look not only in your life, but all around the world...My Spirt is moving..."***

And so, *Miraculous Interventions VIII, Extraordinary Miracles,* was just named. Oh my, it looks like I will be doing a lot of researching in the coming months.

I had dreamed on Easter morning 2018, of land splitting wide open on the east side of Tennessee, like an earthquake, with bright light rising out of the earth and into the heavens. Then huge cracks all over the earth had started. A light shone simultaneously from everywhere, reaching to the third heaven. It seemed as close as ever to coming true. Revelation? The Holy Spirit was moving like lightening!

See you in the next book!

Love,

Deb

*"**Who** shall separate us
from the love of Christ?
Shall tribulation, or distress
or persecution, or famine,
or nakedness, or peril, or sword?*

*   **Nay**, in all these things
        we are more than conquerors
        through Him that loved us.
        For I am persuaded that
        neither death, or life
        nor angels, nor principalities,
        nor powers, nor things present,
        nor things to come,
        nor height, nor depth,
        nor any other creature,
        shall be able to separate us
        from the love of God,
        which is in
        Christ Jesus Our Lord."*

Romans 8:35, 37-39

We welcome you readers to share your comments and experiences with us like-minded believers. These in this book have been written down in order to encourage the brethren and inspire the secular world.

To contact us, send your e-mail to:
peyronsinjesus@yahoo.com

or to the publisher at:
HomeCraftedArtistry@yahoo.com

Or by US Mail to:
Home Crafted Artistry & Printing
1252 Beechwood Avenue
New Albany, IN 47150

Like us on facebook:
Deborah Aubrey-Peyron, author

Follow Deborah on twitter:
Twitter.com/MiraculousBooks

MORE BOOKS FROM
HOME CRAFTED ARTISTRY & PRINTING:

A Heart for Truth, The Story of Nicodemus
By Joyce Cordell

A Journey of Thought
By Robert W. Bibb

Across the Generations
By Ruth Louise Hayes Williams

Albert's Song
Dr. Stephen E. Ellis

Darkest Knight
Dr. Stephen E. Ellis

Echo Beach
By Nancy Parsons

Fantastic Snowflakes!
Mary Dow Bibb Smith

Hell Is Waiting
Dr. Stephen E. Ellis

His Beauty Unveiled
By Anita K. Bube

Holy Spirit Tours: Winter Excursion I
By Bob Garvey, MR Ed, MA

Lines Fallen in Pleasant Places
(Color or Black and White editions)
Louise Lewis Hill

One Step Closer
By Geri Manning

Nature's Four Seasons
By Julie Whittenberg

Stand Straight and Grow Tall
By Dolores Howell

Sunday Mass, What's It All About?
By Robert W. Bibb

HOME CRAFTED ARTISTRY & PRINTING IN CONJUNCTION WITH ALPHA PUBLISHING BY CAROL GOODMAN HEIZER, M.ED.

Snapshots of Life from a Writer's View

Seasons of a Woman's Life

Losing Your Child, Finding Your Way

Losing Your Child, Finding Your Way Workbook

www.ingramcontent.com/pod-product-compliance
Lightning Source LLC
Chambersburg PA
CBHW031959040426
42448CB00006B/423